FIVE QUESTIONS OF CHRISTMAS

— FIVE —
QUESTIONS
of Christmas

* *Unlocking the Mystery* *

ROB BURKHART

ABINGDON PRESS

NASHVILLE

FIVE QUESTIONS OF CHRISTMAS
UNLOCKING THE MYSTERY

Copyright © 2015 by Robin Burkhart

All rights reserved.

Macro Editor: Lauren Winner

Published in association with Credo Communications.

Library of Congress Cataloging-in-Publication Data

Burkhart, Rob.
Five questions of Christmas : unlocking the mystery / Rob Burkhart.—First [edition].
     pages cm
     ISBN 978-1-6308-8129-0 (binding: soft back)   1. Jesus Christ—Nativity.
I. Title.
     BT315.3.B87 2015
     232.92—dc23

2015020254

15 16 17 18 19 20 21 22 23 24—10 9 8 7 6 5 4 3 2 1
MANUFACTURED IN THE UNITED STATES OF AMERICA

CONTENTS

CONTENTS

Christmas 1990

A pile of turkey bones and a solitary dinner roll were the only leftovers from our delicious Christmas dinner. My parents' old house was full of people and presents and the joyful chaos of a large, loving family.

In the kitchen, my mom and sisters chatted and laughed while washing dishes and putting them away. My brother and brothers-in-law talked and kept an eye on the younger children playing with their new toys while the television no one was watching flickered with images of Scrooge and Marley's ghost. Outside in the yard, the older kids threw snowballs, tussled, and laughed in the snow.

My father sat at the head of the dining room table, his place at the table, the perfect vantage point for observing his busy brood of children and grandchildren. He leaned back in his chair, shoulders slightly rounded with age, hands wrapped around his coffee mug. I poured my own cup of coffee, sweet and light, and slid into the chair next to Dad. I expected him to tease me about not drinking my coffee black. But he didn't.

We sat silently for a few minutes. I watched the snow fall on the corn stubble in the field across the road. Dad continued to study the joyous panorama of his family. A look of deep satisfaction stretched across his face. He smiled and said to me, "Your mom and me, we did good. We did real good!" ·

Dad raised his cup for another sip of dark coffee. A deep breath faded into a contented sigh, and he smiled again. For just a moment I felt of twinge of fear: would I feel as content looking back over my life? I wasn't sure.

PROLOGUE

WHAT'S HAPPENED TO CHRISTMAS?

These memories represent just one Christmas from the dozens I've celebrated in my lifetime, but it was one of the sweetest I recall. Three generations of my family gathered to celebrate Christ's birth, exchange gifts, and share a hearty meal. It wasn't perfect or fancy, but we were all together. We loved one another deeply and that's what mattered most.

Sadly, Christmas does not always evoke such pleasant memories. In my own life, some Christmases were hard. There were years when it was too expensive or time consuming to travel, so a telephone call replaced a warm personal visit. Some years an unoccupied dining room chair was a painful reminder of military deployment, a transfer to assisted living, or a recent death. It's hard to gather around the table when one dearly loved and sorely missed is missing.

For the retail industry, the Friday after Thanksgiving launches a frenzy of shopping and profit making set to the continual blare of holiday songs. For churches and charitable organizations,

Advent is a season of giving and a final push for solvency before the end of the tax year. For businesses and employees, December brings the hope that corporate success will parlay into personal compensation, holiday bonuses, and salary increases.

Regardless of their motivations, billions of people around the world observe Christmas, give gifts, and celebrate. For most, Christmas has little or nothing to do with Jesus. Somehow this celebration of a Christian holy day has become a worldwide secular holiday. Global media, online communications, and the export of American consumerism deliver a shiny Hollywood version of Christmas with celebrity-sung carols, artificial snow, and twinkling lights. It brought surfing Santas to Sydney, reindeer to Beijing, and jingle bells to Johannesburg. Extravagant holiday displays illuminate shopping malls from Houston to Hong Kong to Helsinki.

Don't get me wrong; I have nothing against reindeer cookies, Christmas trees, or even Santa. But the singing snowmen, shiny tinsel, and door-buster sales can obscure the real Christmas story.

> In those days a decree went out from Emperor Augustus that all the world should be registered. This was the first registration and was taken while Quirinius was governor of Syria. All went to their own towns to be registered. Joseph also went from the town of Nazareth in Galilee to Judea, to the city of David called Bethlehem, because he was de-

4

scended from the house and family of David. He went to be registered with Mary, to whom he was engaged and who was expecting a child. While they were there, the time came for her to deliver her child. And she gave birth to her first-born son and wrapped him in bands of cloth, and laid him in a manger, because there was no place for them in the inn. (Luke 2:1-7)

This quiet event, sometime around 4 BCE, changed history. Beneath the trappings, Christmas is the story of an unmarried, pregnant teenager, her brokenhearted fiancé, and the birth of her little boy. This baby born in humble surroundings to poor parents grew into an extraordinary and grace-filled man. His wise teachings and remarkable sacrifice transformed cultures and impacted the lives of billions.

Who Jesus was has been a source of controversy since that first Christmas. Contemporary opinions are as different as the people who hold them. People think about him, his mission in the world, and his teachings in vastly different ways. Nor is there any real agreement on his place in history. Some believe he is the most important person to ever live. Others think he has little or no place in our modern world. But the baby born in a manger still generates worldwide attention. Despite our incredible cultural diversity and different celebrations, people feel united during the Christmas season. Families gather, coworkers attend parties, neighbors exchange baked goods. Even nations determined to destroy each other have issued cease-fires to stop their wars at Christmas. The question is, why? The most compelling answers aren't found in Christmas parties, holiday concerts, or shopping malls but in the hearts and minds of people universally drawn to the story. Somehow we recognize our longings, our dreams, and ourselves in Jesus' story. We find reasons to hope in a hopeless world and a light in the dark night of despair. Trapped in our current reality, we find the strength to strive for a better and brighter future. This child who refused to be defined by his questionable birth, lowly status, or poverty inspires us to find answers to life's most troubling questions.

The Gospel writers Luke and Matthew recount five questions in the stories surrounding the birth of Jesus that open the door to life's great mysteries. I first noticed the five Christmas questions while preparing a Christmas devotional lesson. The questions helped me think about the story and its people very differently. In the years that followed, I've reflected on their meaning and significance. It is interesting that the birth of Jesus is surrounded not only with pronouncements and prayers and declarations (though there are those, too) but also with questions.

Questions, after all, invite a response. They are an especially engaging form of speech welcoming everyone who hears the question to ponder, think, reflect, mull—and risk his or her own answer. Questions draw us in—and the questions surrounding Jesus' birth draw us into the great Christmas mystery. Each one of these questions is an invitation for us to enter into the story, and make it our own.

Zechariah, the father of John the Baptist, asked, "How will I know that this is so?" (Luke 1:18). As a priest and scholar, Zechariah searched for truth. But when given an unexpected and improbable blessing, his first response was mistrust. We all look for something we can trust as we struggle in the shifting sands of doubt.

Mary, the mother of Jesus, asked, "How can this be?" (Luke 1:34). Mary was given a bizarre divine assignment laced with scandal and shame. Her unexplainable pregnancy was punishable by death according to the Jewish law. Like us, Mary faced an incredible and potentially tragic challenge.

Elizabeth, the mother of John the Baptist, asked, "Why has this happened to me?" (Luke 1:43). For years, Elizabeth's barrenness was evidence of God's disfavor or neglect. Now in her old age God gave her an extravagant blessing: according to the angel's testimony, her miracle child would become a prophet. That wasn't fair either. We all struggle with the inherent unfairness of life.

The people witnessing the naming ceremony for Zechariah's infant son, John, asked, "What then will this child become?" (Luke 1:66). They wondered about the future of this unique child, born to elderly parents and given an unlikely name. But they could not have fathomed the eccentric ministry and brutal execution of John the Baptizer. We all peer down the long tunnel of time and wonder what the future will bring.

The magi, a group of wise men from the east, followed a star and asked, "Where is the child?" (Matthew 2:2). Their quest for a newborn King of the Jews was longer and stranger than they anticipated. Like the magi, we search for meaning and purpose in life and often come away unsatisfied

The Nativity stories pose these five deep questions, inviting us in—but they also contain answers. If we unwrap these stories, we find that Zechariah, Mary, Elizabeth, the crowd, and the magi found answers to their dilemmas. Along the way they developed resilience, conviction, gratitude, creativity, and faith. We can find answers to our most troubling questions and a map that leads to a richer life and a lasting legacy.

Many don't believe Jesus is the Son of God and ignore these deep issues. But that doesn't mean the questions aren't real. Some people prefer the false comfort of an unexamined life to the richer life that comes from deep and difficult reflection. They choose the cocoon of the status quo rather than risk transformation and a soul set free. That's their choice. Others are willing to explore this difficult terrain to find answers and even transformation.

Jesus faced these deep and confounding questions. He dealt with injustice, tragedy, and uncertainty. Unlike most people, Jesus faced these questions with unflinching courage, openness, and determination. He lived an extraordinary life that serves as a blueprint for all who seek answers to life's most challenging questions.

Historically, Christians have believed the Bible is the inspired word of God and the infallible rule of faith and practice. Other readers of Scripture see the Bible as a collection of ancient wisdom to be considered carefully, but not taken literally. Some people have little or no exposure to or experience with the Bible. However one finally views the Scriptures, it makes sense for anyone seeking answers to life's urgent questions to read the Bible and explore its ancient wisdom. The Bible includes questions, and answers, and questions again. Perhaps these questions were included in these stories because people in every generation ask them.

Ancient wisdom and sacred texts abound. It's popular to say that they all convey the same distilled wisdom of the ages and the sages. But do they?

I believe the Bible is unique in its ability to speak to human longings and the human condition with ultimate wisdom and truth. Christians can and do respect and appreciate the wisdom of other traditions and religions. They provide mirrors of the human soul and tell stories of our common quest. But in the end, they are man's conversation about the Divine. The Bible is God's conversation with man.

We need wisdom beyond contemporary culture, temporary assumptions, or a vague spiritual mélange. This truth cannot be ferreted out by human wisdom or clever sophistry, discovered like a physical law, or tested like a scientific hypothesis. Only God, whose power is great, whose wisdom is perfect, whose love is absolute, and whose scope is eternal, can reveal ultimate truth.

But we will have to dig deeper, to look beyond the Christmas pageants and happy holiday animations. We'll have to reexamine the Nativity stories with a treasure hunter's eye for clues. We'll need courage to question assumptions and a dose of humility to accept surprise twists.

But why? Why should we pause and look past the holiday tinsel and the Christmas card theology to meditate again on the baby in the manger and the stories of his birth?

Over the centuries, many people have found that the God of the Christmas story is part of their story too. Emmanuel, the God who is with us, gave people the courage to fight for justice and the strength to endure hardship. Emmanuel, the God who is with us, brought tranquility to chaos and hope to hardship. Emmanuel, the God who is with us, brought peace to contentious relationships and restoration to broken lives. And this same God promises to be with us today and every day of our lives.

True treasure indeed!

There are people who ask these questions and don't like the answers. Maybe you won't. I didn't for a long time. But for just a moment, imagine discovering the sweeping grandeur of a truth so sublime and beautiful that life actually makes sense. What if we can truly satisfy our deepest longings? What if there is someone we can wholeheartedly believe in? What if suffering and tragedy aren't just painful and meaningless experiences, but the raw material of a rich, beautiful, and well-lived life? What if we could face the future with the bright hope of real joy? What if the Christmas story really brought peace on earth and goodwill to all?

Just imagine...

CHAPTER 1

HOW WILL I KNOW?

Zechariah's Journey from Mistrust to Conviction

Each of the four Gospels tells the story of Jesus—Jesus' life, his teachings, his death at the hands of the Roman government and their co-conspirators in the Jewish Sanhedrin. Although each of the Gospels is in some sense a "biography" of Jesus, only Matthew and Luke mention his birth. The most detailed Nativity story is in the Gospel of Luke 1 and 2. Luke intentionally gathered eyewitness accounts and carefully researched his stories. His goal was to tell the story of Jesus in a trustworthy and straightforward way that both Jews and Gentiles would understand. Luke wanted his readers to see how God's promises were fulfilled through Jesus.

Luke begins his Gospel account with two of Jesus' relatives, a priest named Zechariah and his wife, Elizabeth.

> In the days of King Herod of Judea, there was a priest
> named Zechariah, who belonged to the priestly order of
> Abijah. His wife was a descendant of Aaron, and her name
> was Elizabeth. Both of them were righteous before God,
> living blamelessly according to all the commandments and
> regulations of the Lord. But they had no children, because
> Elizabeth was barren, and both were getting on in years.
> (Luke 1:5-7)

Zechariah and his wife, Elizabeth, were known for their personal holiness and obedience to God's commandments. Despite
their righteousness, Zechariah and Elizabeth were childless. They
were like the other barren couples in Scripture who became the
patriarchs and matriarchs of faith: Abraham and Sarah (Genesis 11), Isaac and Rebekah (Genesis 25), and Jacob and Rachel
(Genesis 30). God kept His promise that Abraham's offspring
would be like the stars, so numerous that no one could count
them (Genesis 15:5-6), despite infertility and even menopause.
God *could* open wombs, but God hadn't for this couple. There
was no miracle child toddling around Zechariah and Elizabeth's
house, getting into the kitchen cupboards.

> Once when [Zechariah] was serving as priest before God
> and his section was on duty, he was chosen by lot, accord-
> ing to the custom of the priesthood, to enter the sanctu-
> ary of the Lord and offer incense. Now at the time of the

incense offering, the whole assembly of the people was praying outside. Then there appeared to him an angel of the Lord, standing at the right side of the altar of incense. When Zechariah saw him, he was terrified; and fear overwhelmed him. (Luke 1:8-12)

Zechariah is in the midst of this extremely important assignment in the most sacred part of the temple. A crowd of people are praying and waiting outside. Suddenly an angel appears. Zechariah is absolutely terrified. After all, he knows the stories of priests who were struck dead for doing their job incorrectly (Leviticus 10; Numbers 16). But instead of judgment, the angel Gabriel delivers a special message from God.

But the angel said to him, "Do not be afraid, Zechariah, for your prayer has been heard. Your wife Elizabeth will bear you a son, and you will name him John. You will have joy and gladness, and many will rejoice at his birth, for he will be great in the sight of the Lord. He must never drink wine or strong drink; even before his birth he will be filled with the Holy Spirit. He will turn many of the people of Israel to the Lord their God. With the spirit and power of Elijah he will go before him, to turn the hearts of parents to their children, and the disobedient to the wisdom of the righteous, to make ready a people prepared for the Lord." (Luke 1:13-17)

It was a truly unanticipated announcement. Although there was, as we have seen, precedent in earlier biblical stories for just this kind of miracle, there had been no prophets or prophesies for four hundred years. And now there's an angel with a personalized message from God: Elizabeth will bear a son who will bring joy to many people and be great in the sight of the Lord. This was completely outside Zechariah's understanding of how the world worked.

Zechariah had no expectation of miraculous offspring. He and Elizabeth had prayed for children since they were newlyweds. Each month their hopes soared and then soured. Their youth and middle age were gone, and now it was too late. Elizabeth's biological clock had stopped ticking. They were elderly and childless. Why would God answer their prayer with a miracle child now? But this announcement is much bigger than Zechariah and Elizabeth. The angel said this miracle son would be a great prophet like Elijah who would prepare God's people for the coming of the Messiah. That was even more unbelievable news! On that day Zechariah may have been afraid to get his hopes up. Maybe he couldn't face one more steep drop on his emotional roller coaster. Maybe he was afraid to believe his dream could come true. But Zechariah wasn't prepared to trust his future or his hopes and dreams to anyone, not even an angel.

Given all this, Zechariah's skepticism of both the messenger and the message seems warranted, even justified. The angel's prediction impacted his own family and all the Jewish people. It was terrifying to have these deep desires for a child and a Messiah exposed to anyone, even an angel. Surely Zechariah is allowed a moment of doubt or a question for clarification. Zechariah gathers his courage and finds his voice.

> Zechariah said to the angel, "How will I know that this is so? For I am an old man, and my wife is getting on in years." The angel replied, "I am Gabriel. I stand in the presence of God, and I have been sent to speak to you and to bring you this good news. But now, because you did not believe my words, which will be fulfilled in their time, you will become mute, unable to speak, until the day these things occur." (Luke 1:18-20)

Gabriel doesn't appreciate having his integrity questioned. He was sent from the presence of God to deliver this message of good news. Mission accomplished. Unlike Samson's parents who received multiple clarifications about their Nazirite child (Judges 13), Zechariah's parental pronouncement comes to a screeching halt. Gabriel leaves.

> Meanwhile the people were waiting for Zechariah, and wondered at his delay in the sanctuary. When he did come out, he could not speak to them, and they realized that he had seen a vision in the sanctuary. He kept motioning to

them and remained unable to speak. When his time of service was ended, he went to his home. (Luke 1:21-23)

Zechariah leaves the temple in silence. The crowd sees that he's noticeably altered by his angelic encounter. Mysteriously mute, he uses gestures to communicate the unimaginable news. Somehow he finishes his responsibilities and then travels back to his home in the Judean hills. He and Elizabeth keep a low profile as God's promise takes form. "After those days his wife Elizabeth conceived, and for five months she remained in seclusion. She said, 'This is what the Lord has done for me when he looked favorably on me and took away the disgrace I have endured among my people'" (Luke 1:24-25).

A Matter of Trust

Zechariah's situation crystallizes the questions everyone asks: How will I know that this is so? How can I be sure? Whom can I trust?

Trust is so pervasive and necessary that we become oblivious to it. In countless encounters each day we trust our family and friends, our business colleagues, and service providers. Our answer to the question, "How can I be sure?" sets the course of our lives. Will we be open and adventurous or fearful and defensive? It depends on trust.

Every investor looks for a stable portfolio that protects capital and reaps dividends. Every spouse wants a marriage that holds firm in good times and bad. Every employee wants to work for a company that is fair and reputable. In all these arenas and many more people seek a safe harbor, a place that can weather life's inevitable storms.

Meanwhile, voices all around us shout, "Trust me!" We trust particular political candidates and financial institutions. We put faith in doctors, schoolteachers, airline pilots, and restaurant cooks. We trust people we'll never meet—elevator inspectors, software developers, and utility workers. From the day we are born, trust infuses our daily lives. People learn early whether they are safe, protected, and cared for and whether they can trust their world and those in it. According to some psychologists, this is the first thing we learn: the child in the crib, hungry, wet, and miserable can only cry. And the child learns about how to trust, whom to trust—whether to trust—from what happens after the child cries. If a loving and caring adult responds with a dry diaper, a bottle, a gentle voice, and a loving touch, the child learns that she is safe and that other people can be trusted. An angry, cursing, or uncaring visage and rough handling teaches the child that the world is a dangerous place and people are not to be trusted.

Emotional or physical abandonment or neglect damages a child's ability to trust. The child learns that he or she is not important, is of little or no value, and may grow to feel unworthy of love, care, and protection. These children lose the ability to trust others and come to believe that they must take care of themselves because no one else will.

Trampled Trust

Trust is risky business. Even if we grow up in a home brimming with love and care, someone will eventually break our trust. Someone we thought trustworthy lies, betrays, cheats, abandons, or abuses. In those moments we learn to withhold our trust and protect ourselves.

Knowing when to withhold trust is essential to avoiding vulnerability and risk. People learn to recognize and respect their gut instincts. Ignoring your intuition opens the door to unexpected and sometimes disastrous results. Not trusting the too-good-to-be-true infomercial saves money, aggravation, and disappointment. Not trusting the old rickety ladder prevents broken bones and medical bills. That isn't pathological. It's prudent.

But in its extreme forms, distrust creates disastrous results. Relationships are ruined by suspicion and jealousy. One's decision-making ability is paralyzed by fear, skepticism, and misgivings. This deep distrust no longer protects. It becomes a personalized prison.

Conundrum

Trust is a conundrum.

Our simultaneous need for trust and safety requires a fine-tuned balance. Excessive trust creates gullible fools or vulnerable victims. Obsessive safeguarding leads to paranoid vigilantes or homebound hermits. We need to find a spot between the two extremes.

Not everything is as it appears. Some people we encounter are bold-faced liars, con artists, and manipulators. But breaking trust is not always intentional or malicious. People may not have the courage to protect us or the persistence needed to keep their commitment. Maybe they are selfish or overwhelmed by their own needs. They might be unhelpful, oblivious, or ignorant. Regardless of the reason, we are let down. We lose a little faith in humanity. We withdraw our trust. "Like a bad tooth or a lame foot is trust in a faithless person in time of trouble" (Proverbs 25:19).

This struggle with trust is not new. In every era, humans create societal guidelines and interact with the natural world. The paradigms change with culture, experience, and time. Much of this received wisdom proves false in the end. The certainties of one generation soon become rejected notions and quaint anachronisms. But for some people these changes are devastating and terrifying. What seemed like bedrock truth is only shifting sand. "There is a way that seems right to a person, but its end is the way to death" (Proverbs 14:12).

Like a person who's drowning, we frantically look around for assistance. We grab possessions, hoping they'll be a life preserver to keep us afloat. We latch on to other people hoping they'll be the lifeguards who pull us back to shore. We cling to theories, philosophies, and programs like a boat that will get us to our destination. There are innumerable things we trust that cannot save us.

Some people trust money. They use financial wealth and material possessions as a hedge against the destructive forces of life. Money gives you access to better education, medical care, and safe neighborhoods. Money can help you influence others and champion your causes. But money cannot make you truly safe, no matter how much wealth you stockpile. Economic systems fail, natural disasters strike, and tragedies happen. In the rubble left by the 2011 tsunami in Japan, rescue workers found safes containing millions in cash. Their owners believed that wealth and their possessions gave them security. But the wealthiest died with the poorest that day. Mansions and hovels were swept away together. Money cannot be trusted. "Those who trust in their riches will wither, but the righteous will flourish like green leaves" (Proverbs 11:28).

Some people trust power. Being part of a group—a labor union, a political party, a club, or a gang—is one way to exert power and control. At the national scale, political and military powers look intimidating. No one denies that those with power ·impose their will on those without it and use power to protect themselves from the circumstance and consequences of life. Most of the time, powerful trumps powerless in the game of life. But much of life is beyond the control of anyone no matter how powerful they are. Trusting power is deceptive.

In Zechariah's time most people would have trusted the all-powerful Roman Empire, not Zechariah's wild-eyed son—the wilderness prophet with his strange clothes and even stranger diet. Nor would they have gambled on his cousin, the poor carpenter and wandering rabbi from Nazareth. Both died at the hands of the rich and powerful.

Two thousand years later, billions revere the baptizer and the carpenter. The great and powerful of their day are remembered as mere bit players in Jesus and John's story. Soldiers of the cross have replaced the great Roman legions that once trampled every adversary but have been relegated to the dusty pages of history and unmarked graves.

> Do not put your trust in princes,
>> in mortals, in whom there is no help.
> When their breath departs, they return to the earth;
>> on that very day their plans perish. (Psalm 146:3-4)

Some people trust possessions. They obsess over the latest fashions, the fastest cars, or the newest technology. They collect music, movies, shoes, art, or souvenirs. They accumulate belongings at a rapid pace while their basements, garages, and storage facilities overflow. At some point, their idolatry is exposed. Their possessions are put on display at garage sales and estate auctions like cadavers in a morgue, lifeless and decaying. Neighbors marvel at how much clutter was packed in the house. Adult children sort the idolatrous debris of their parents' lives, wondering why they spent so much time and money on such things.

> Their idols are like scarecrows in a cucumber field,
>> and they cannot speak;
> they have to be carried,
>> for they cannot walk.
> Do not be afraid of them,
>> for they cannot do evil,
>>> nor is it in them to do good.
> (Jeremiah 10:5)

Some people trust idols and heroes. They fixate on athletes, celebrities, and charismatic leaders. They idealize their families and friends. Their worship isn't religious, but it commands extravagant and excessive devotion. Idol worship is the passionate fervor that permeates sports arenas and concert venues. It's the shimmering tributes at the funerals of public figures and family members. Underneath this idol worship is a transaction: loyalty and devotion in exchange for attention and affection. The worshipers are exhilarated by their idol experiences and crave more. Eventually the idol disappoints, the thrill fades, and the worshipers move on to their next obsession. "All who make idols are nothing, and the things they delight in do not profit; their witnesses neither see nor know. And so they will be put to shame" (Isaiah 44:9).

Some people trust only themselves. They pour their energy

and concentration into their careers, their physiques, their academic credentials, and their accolades. But someday soon, our toned bodies will weaken, our shiny trophies will tarnish, and our sharp minds will fail. We are not indestructible nor immortal.

> What they trust in is fragile;
> > what they rely on is a spider's web.
> They lean on the web, but it gives way;
> > they cling to it, but it does not hold.
> (Job 8:14-15 NIV)

But nothing can remove our primal need for trust. Woven deep into the fabric of every life is the need for someone or something to believe in.

The problem isn't our need for trust. It's what we choose to trust.

This deep conundrum about trust—our deep need *to* trust, and yet the many times we've learned that what we want to trust is only partially trustworthy—is what Zechariah's question expressed. Whom can I trust? And how can I know that the one I trust is worthy of that trust?

The Main Things

Zechariah and Elizabeth's lives progressed just as the angel foretold. "After those days his wife Elizabeth conceived, and for five months she remained in seclusion. She said, 'This is what the Lord has done for me when he looked favorably on me and took away the disgrace I have endured among my people'" (Luke 1:24-25 CEB).

What can we learn about trust from Zechariah's journey?

First, trust is possible. The notion that trust can be earned is a myth. To earn something is to do the work or pay the price. Trust has no price. If it had a price it would cost more than anyone could pay. If trust could be earned it would mean that once the price is paid and the standard is met, trust would be automatic. It never, ever happens that way.

To earn trust someone would have to be flawlessly trustworthy. No one is in that category. No one is without failure or fault. No one has the power to always accomplish everything he or she promises. There is only one exception and people don't trust him.

Trust cannot be earned but it can be given. We can find the courage and strength to choose trust and triumph over our fear, to risk and reap the rewards, and to experience the joy of living beyond the limits of our experience.

Second, trust is precious. As a priest, Zechariah knew God's copious laws and how hard it was to follow them. But this wasn't a human standing in front of him, it was an angelic messenger sent from heaven. Zechariah was face to face with perfection, and that made his trepidation unnecessary and unwarranted. Zechariah withheld his absolute trust from Gabriel and he paid a high price for his doubt.

Trust is a precious gift from one person to another. By trusting we make ourselves vulnerable, and in intimate relationships reveal the deep things held in our hearts and minds.

When we are trusted we are given one of the greatest gifts anyone can bestow on another. We are made guardians of the hopes, dreams, and future of another.

Third, trust has great potential. Through credibility and reliability, we extend increasing amounts of trust. Suppose you need to find a trustworthy mechanic or babysitter or physician. You start by asking your friends whom they recommend. You investigate the person's reputation and check his or her references. You give that person a small assignment and watch how he or she handles it—an oil change, a few hours with your children, a basic checkup. If the person meets our standards, we entrust him or her with more.

Trusting relationships enrich our lives financially, emotionally, relationally, and spiritually. We achieve more, experience greater joy, and discover the wonders of life together. Without trust we lose all that is possible when we partner with others whether it is in friendship, marriage, or business. Trust has the power to heal broken relationships, set us free from our past failures, and lets us begin again.

Fourth, we can make trust more predictable. Based on our experience and observations, we judge if someone or something is reliable. We store up positive encounters and begin to extend our loyalty. Prior experience is a decent predictor of future trustworthiness. Nowadays, recommendations and reviews are everywhere. We consult consumer ratings before making a major purchase and pick contractors from prescreened lists. We would rather trust in the opinions of strangers than make a mistake.

How we live and conduct our day-to-day lives makes the gift of trust more or less predictable. If we prove unreliable and unfaithful, we lose trust and destroy the relationship. If we live dependable, honest, and loyal lives, we are more likely to be given and keep the trust of others. We cannot earn their trust, but by being reliable we make it more likely.

The Triumph of Trust

In the turmoil of modern life, finding a solid place to stand isn't easy. But we all have to stand somewhere. The challenge is to rightly trust and then act rightly on that trust.

Most of the time we use our senses to figure things out the best we can. Reality is what we know through our senses and our science. It is a physical, external world governed by laws we can count on even when we don't understand them. It is the hard, unyielding reality of the physical universe, of cause and effect, of trial and error, and the scientific method. We trust it.

The fact we can't trust human nature is part of that solid reality. Eons of experience and the wisdom of generations prove the predictability of nature and that people aren't predictable. That conclusion isn't based on mystical insights from another world. It's the hard reality people have faced ever since there were people and Cain murdered Abel.

The Book of Genesis contains a steady stream of unpleasant plot twists: betrayal, disobedience, jealousy, murder, rape, debauchery, and destruction. God created people, and people created chaos.

Miraculous events throughout the Bible stretch the boundaries of reality. A virgin gives birth, a man walks on water, five thousand people are fed with one boy's lunch, and a blind man is healed with spit and mud. That doesn't sound like the real world we know. We can't explain or measure how miracles happen relying on the normal ways we understand the world.

The second way to understand reality goes beyond the five senses and the physical world. It is the unseen, mysterious, miraculous, and an inexplicable force that tugs at reality.

The world is full of people who believe in something beyond what is seen. Humans have countless ways of perceiving and describing the Divine. They envision a powerful creator, Supreme Being, absentee landlord, benevolent parent, harsh taskmaster, universal spirit, or infinite essence. Some people believe in one god while others have multiple deities. Others see themselves as spiritual but not religious and reject these notions of God altogether.

Some people's religious beliefs lead them to sequester themselves in cloistered communities, while others intentionally interact with the world as much as possible. Some people ignore the spiritual world except at holidays or in moments of crisis. Others are relentlessly motivated by trying to please God, whether out of guilt or true devotion. Most people hedge their bets. They're not entirely sure the spiritual realm exists, but they go along with the rites or practices of their culture. They want to enjoy life's pleasures, but not offend any deities lurking out of sight.

The Christmas story presents a vastly different way to understand life and reality than either of these. This third way combines the physical with the spiritual. This perspective sees human history as the story of God who created the world and loves it completely. Estranged from humanity by our sin, God goes to great lengths to save humankind when Jesus comes to earth on a stealth rescue mission. God welcomes prodigals back home with compassion, love, and grace. God wars against evil and malevolent forces that steal, kill, and destroy humanity and creation.

That's the real Christmas story, the story of Jesus. Millions have built their lives trusting this salvation story. They believe God provides the one true foundation of life and God can always be trusted. Entrusting our lives to the God of the Christmas story means we can deal with life's challenges, uncertainties, and fear.

Fear is an internal reaction to an external circumstance. It is our natural response to a threat, whether something real or imagined. Healthy fear protects us from impending danger, unreasonable risks, and destructive choices. Healthy fear is good and we should respect it. Sometimes the fear we feel is the hand of God, sparing and protecting us.

But there's also an unhealthy fear, as we learned earlier. It's the fear that isolates, immobilizes, intimidates, and overpowers. It is irrational and unnecessary fear. Unhealthy fear cripples our initiative and hinders us from achieving our goals. The antidote to excessive fear is having the courage to trust and love. But how?

First, we stand up to fear by assessing the situation. Are my motives in line with God's justice, love, and compassion? Or are my motives shallow, selfish, and hurtful? If our undertaking is truly valuable and right, we can trust in God's power. We can act with courage and conviction. The Bible contains dozens of affirmations and admonitions for personal fortitude.

> Moses said to the people, "Do not be afraid, stand firm, and see the deliverance that the LORD will accomplish for you today." (Exodus 14:13)
> "I hereby command you: Be strong and courageous; do not be frightened or dismayed, for the LORD your God is with you wherever you go." (Joshua 1:9)

Second, we stand up to fear by accepting consequences. Doing the right thing doesn't mean things will go your way. In fact, they probably won't. People who fight for justice may end up in the justice system. The Apostle Paul wrote many of his letters from prison while waiting to be executed. Throughout history, believers have been persecuted, beaten, shunned, and martyred for their beliefs. We must press on even when we are pushed back.

Jesus said, "Blessed are those who are persecuted for righteousness' sake, for theirs is the kingdom of heaven. Blessed are you when people revile you and persecute you and utter all kinds of evil against you falsely on my account. Rejoice and be glad, for your reward is great in heaven, for in the same way they persecuted the prophets who were before you" (Matthew 5:10-12).

Third, we stand up to fear by acknowledging it. The only thing worse than facing our fears is not facing them. When you push fear down, it comes back up. The fear you thought was concealed is now bigger, stronger, and more destructive. Irrational fear smothers the soul and whispers doubt in your ear. We can stand up to fear because we are loved and protected by God. "Discipline yourselves, keep alert. Like a roaring lion your adversary the devil prowls around, looking for someone to devour. Resist him, steadfast in your faith, for you know that your brothers and sisters in all the world are undergoing the same kinds of suffering" (1 Peter 5:8-9).

Fourth, we stand up to fear by facing opposition. No great thing is ever accomplished without facing opposition. Jesus' vision of justice and equality receives plenty of resistance from the powers of the world. Some objections are polite, civil, pleasantly wrapped requests for you to stop. They cajole and coax people to back down or change their minds. Other objections are raw, violent, and ugly. Your life may be threatened. This is why we admire the signers of the American Declaration of Independence and freedom fighters like Martin Luther King Jr., Nelson Mandela, and Rosa Parks. They risked everything for a better future beyond what they could see. "For our struggle is not against enemies of blood and flesh, but against the rulers, against the authorities, against the cosmic powers of this present darkness, against the spiritual forces of evil in the heavenly places. Therefore take up the whole armor of God, so that you may be able to withstand on that evil day, and having done everything, to stand firm" (Ephesians 6:12-13).

Finally, we stand up to fear by allowing it to change us. There is an upside to fear: it helps us identify what really matters. Fear strengthens our convictions and helps uncover the ideals we value most at the core of our identity. If we stand firm in our beliefs when we are challenged, we develop integrity and confidence. We stand on a solid foundation with the courage to withstand increasingly dangerous situations. Such courage is the stuff of heroes. "May you be made strong with all the strength that comes from his glorious power, and may you be prepared to endure everything with patience, while joyfully giving thanks to the Father, who has enabled you to share in the inheritance of the saints in the light" (Colossians 1:11-12).

Standing Firm

Zechariah and Elizabeth's nine months of watching and waiting came to an end. Both their baby and their faith were fully formed.

Now the time came for Elizabeth to give birth, and she bore a son. Her neighbors and relatives heard that the Lord had shown his great mercy to her, and they rejoiced with her.

On the eighth day they came to circumcise the child, and they were going to name him Zechariah after his father. But his mother said, "No; he is to be called John." They said to her, "None of your relatives has this name." Then they began motioning to his father to find out what name he wanted to give him. He asked for a writing tablet and wrote, "His name is John." And all of them were amazed. Immediately his mouth was opened and his tongue freed, and he began to speak, praising God. (Luke 1:57-64)

Zechariah and Elizabeth held their ground against their neighbors and the cultural norms that insisted their child have a family name. They stood on faith that their child was a miraculous gift with a divinely ordered destiny. They stood with the angel. They stood firm.

Three decades later, their son, John the Baptist, demonstrated the same courage in the face of opposition. He preached repentance to people who didn't want to repent. He challenged political and religious authority and was arrested, languished in Herod's dungeon, and faced an unknown future. But John trusted God's call on his life. He believed that Jesus was the Messiah. He struggled, but John stood firm to the very end. It cost John his life, but truth eventually triumphed.

Zechariah believed God's promises with conviction and confidence. When his long months of silence were finally broken, his first words were full of praise and thanksgiving to God.

> Then his father Zechariah was filled with the Holy Spirit and spoke this prophecy:
> "Blessed be the Lord God of Israel,
>> for he has looked favorably on his people and
>> redeemed them.
> He has raised up a mighty savior for us
>> in the house of his servant David,
> as he spoke through the mouth of his holy prophets
>> from of old,
>> that we would be saved from our enemies and from
>> the hand of all who hate us.
> Thus he has shown the mercy promised to our
>> ancestors,
>> and has remembered his holy covenant,
> the oath that he swore to our ancestor Abraham,
>> to grant us that we, being rescued from the hands
>> of our enemies,
> might serve him without fear, in holiness and
>> righteousness
>> before him all our days." (Luke 1:67-75)

There are moments we are sure of God's great love and care. We are able to rest in challenging and difficult times because we feel deeply God's trustworthiness. At other times we wonder whether or not he is truly trustworthy. There are pieces of life we joyfully trust God with and others we guard jealously, afraid of surrendering even to him. As it turns out, God shows himself trustworthy in all those times through his word. He knows us and loves us when we rest in his care and when we question him. When our wondering selves, our uncertain selves, come back to this story each Christmas, we discover that we have a companion in Zechariah, someone who asks one of the deepest questions of life with us: whom shall I trust?

Questions

1. Sometimes we struggle with trusting others because we want to keep control. Do we truly control our own lives? If so, what do we control?

2. Why is it hard to trust another person? God?

3. What does it take to truly trust? What does the other person have to do? What do you have to do?

4. What place do pride and fear play in our lack of trust in others and in God?

5. People find it harder to admit their need to trust God in some areas of life more than others. What areas do you struggle with? Why do you struggle with them more than other areas?

6. Is it really possible to trust God with only parts of life? Why or why not?

7. What can you do to learn to trust God more?

Christmas 1997

Each afternoon that fall I picked Mark up from school and we rushed home just in time to watch re-runs of *Due South*. It was a show about a displaced Canadian Mountie named Benton Fraser who solved crimes for the Chicago Police Department with Detective Raymond Vecchio with the help of his father's ghost and his deaf wolf-dog name Diefenbaker. It was a funny, quirky show, and we loved watching it together.

At Christmastime I devised a plan: I would make Mark hunt for his biggest present by answering *Due South* trivia questions. To make it harder, the series of clues were spread throughout the house. He was fourteen, and I figured he deserved it.

On Christmas morning we opened all the gifts that were under the tree. Mark tried to be gracious and appreciative, but I could tell the gifts weren't what he really wanted. When everyone was done, I walked over to the mantel and pulled out a small box.

"Merry Christmas, Mark!" I said, handing it to him. He eagerly opened the package and pulled out a piece of paper. "Read it out loud," I said. "We want to know what's going on." As he read the clue, I could see the light bulb go off in his brain. He ran to the front closet, expecting to find his gift. Instead, he found another clue taped to the top shelf.

My wife and I smiled as Mark dashed from room to room, reading out the clues I'd hidden under the basement steps, behind a mounted deer head, inside a kitchen cabinet, beneath the dining room table, and on his favorite ice cream in the basement freezer. The final clue led him to his bedroom. The package was hidden in plain sight beside the camping gear under his bed. "All right!" we heard him shout. He carried it downstairs and joined the rest of the family. I sat down on the floor, leaned against the wall, and watched Mark tear open his present. The gift was exactly what he wanted but could scarcely hope for.

Beaming from ear to ear, Mark stood up and walked over carrying his gift. "Thanks, Dad!"

It was a wonderful Christmas morning!

But our world would be turned upside down all too soon.

In the years that followed, I often thought of that simple and peaceful *Due South* Christmas. I wished it could be that way again, a day of anticipation and gratitude. In the dangerous and dark days of Mark's deployments with the US Marine Corps in Iraq and Afghanistan, we celebrated Christmas half a world apart, and I longed for the boy who found such delight in a game of hide-and-seek. I ached for the joy of having my family sitting around the Christmas tree in a world at peace.

But most of all, I wished that finding what you really wanted was as simple as following clues left by a loving father.

CHAPTER 2

HOW CAN THIS BE?

Mary's Journey from Tragedy to Resilience

Tragedy is an inescapable part of life. It hits us broadside when we least expect it—an accident, diagnosis, natural disaster, health epidemic, or a scandal. Tragedy is never a welcome visitor. When it shows up, we count the moments until it's gone. Tragedy creates turmoil. We wonder what went wrong, what we could have done differently, how it could have been prevented. We wonder why bad things happen and look for meaning in the struggle.

We all want to avoid suffering. But no one can. The challenge isn't to explain suffering. There may be no explanation. Even when there is an explanation it may not help much. Nor is the question of who or what to blame. Blaming doesn't change the facts or bring healing and wholeness. Finally, the issue isn't whether or not we or others deserve to suffer. We may or may not have done things that contribute to our pain. Deserved or undeserved, pain is pain, loss is loss, and a tragedy hurts just as bad. Ultimately, explanations, blame, or guilt can't roll back the clock. What's done is done and our pain is all too real. What we find in the second question of Advent is not a recipe for avoiding tragedy, but a way of converting it—or allowing God to convert it—into goodness.

> In the sixth month the angel Gabriel was sent by God to a town in Galilee called Nazareth, to a virgin engaged to a man whose name was Joseph, of the house of David. The virgin's name was Mary. And he came to her and said, "Greetings, favored one! The Lord is with you." But she was much perplexed by his words and pondered what sort of greeting this might be. The angel said to her, "Do not be afraid, Mary, for you have found favor with God. And now, you will conceive in your womb and bear a son, and you will name him Jesus. He will be great, and will be called the Son of the Most High, and the Lord God will give to him the throne of his ancestor David. He will reign over the house of Jacob forever, and of his kingdom there will be no end." (Luke 1:26-33)

Mary was an ordinary girl. She wasn't wealthy and nothing distinguished her from other peasant girls of her time. Her family is only briefly mentioned in the Gospel genealogies (Matthew 1 and Luke 3). Mary and her fiancé, Joseph, both lived in the village of Nazareth within the province of Galilee on the fringes of the great Roman Empire. The Bible doesn't tell us Mary's exact age, but she was probably in her teens. She probably wasn't well educated. Until the angel showed up, nothing about Mary's life was worthy of history's attention. That's the point.

Church history has painted Mary with a patina of perfection that is immortalized in paintings, statues, and stained glass. It's almost impossible to see the ordinary girl through the halo's glow. Certainly Mary deserves our admiration for her integrity, courage, and obedience. Even God thinks highly of her! But when we first meet Mary, she isn't *theo tokos,* the "God-bearer," carrying the Savior of the world. She was an ordinary young woman getting ready for her wedding.

Mary's response to the angel's pronouncement is remarkable!

> Mary said to the angel, "How can this be, since I am a virgin?" The angel said to her, "The Holy Spirit will come upon you, and the power of the Most High will overshadow you; therefore the child to be born will be holy; he will be called Son of God. And now, your relative Elizabeth in her old age has also conceived a son; and this is the sixth month for her who was said to be barren. For nothing will be impossible with God." Then Mary said, "Here am I, the servant of the Lord; let it be with me according to your word." Then the angel departed from her. (Luke 1:34-38)

Like most people facing something unexpected and potentially tragic, Mary asked, "How can this be?"

In Mary's time and culture, being pregnant and unmarried was more than tragic; it was potentially a death sentence. An unexplainable pregnancy threatened Mary's impending marriage, her physical safety, and her family's reputation. All her relationships and carefully planned future depended on her chastity.

Pregnancy isn't easy to hide, no matter how loose fitting the clothes. Mary's body would change and eventually she would not be able to hide her condition from her parents, family, the people of Nazareth, or her fiancé, Joseph. Who would believe her story about the angel and being history's only pregnant virgin? No one! Well, maybe her relative Elizabeth, who carried her own miracle child.

Tragedy Changes Everything

Tragedy affects every area of a person's life and impacts everyone in it. Anything and everything can change in an instant.

First, tragedy can be a physical threat. A cruel disease, an accident, an inherited condition, and creeping old age can dramatically change a person's body and radically alter a person's life. Our fragile and complex bodies can be damaged by natural disasters, disease, or accidents. Our abilities and mobility are more vulnerable than we realize.

Second, tragedy can threaten our safety and derail our carefully constructed plans. Because she was pregnant but not married, she could be disowned, abandoned, punished, or even stoned to death (Leviticus 20:10). The provision and protection of being someone's daughter or wife would disappear. For us, tragedy can snowball out of control. Unemployment or illness can start a spiral of economic hardship that leads to bankruptcy, foreclosure, and homelessness. The safe havens of our home and neighborhood can disappear in one horrible swoop of misfortune or misjudgment.

Third, tragedy can threaten our relationships. It creates extreme stress that breaks marriages, estranges family members, and destroys friendships. Some people cannot bear to watch a loved one suffer and they leave though they are desperately needed. We feel isolated by the pain and cut off from the very relationship we most need to survive. Tragedy can crack open carefully constructed facades and reveal the ugliness others cannot face. Anger, depression, and self-loathing poison the soil killing a relationship at the root.

Mary's pregnancy endangered her relationships with her parents, future husband, and neighbors. Mary would be alone.

> My heart throbs, my strength fails me;
>> as for the light of my eyes—it also has gone from me.
> My friends and companions stand aloof from my
>> affliction,
>> and my neighbors stand far off.
> (Psalm 38:10-11)

Fourth, tragedy can threaten our self-worth. Suffering often feels like divine judgment and condemnation for our mistakes and bad choices. Even when it isn't our fault, we feel less confident and we downsize our expectations. Mary's pregnancy changed the way people saw her and the way she saw herself. The angel's assurance that she was highly favored might be true in heaven, but it didn't look that way on earth.

> My enemies speak concerning me,
>> and those who watch for my life consult together.
> They say, "Pursue and seize that person
>> whom God has forsaken,
>> for there is no one to deliver."
> O God, do not be far from me;
>> O my God, make haste to help me!
> (Psalm 71:10-12)

Finally, tragedy can threaten our sense of meaning and purpose in life. Mary was going to marry Joseph, be his wife, and raise the children they would have together. The days and years of her life would be filled with the simple joys of making a home for her husband and children. She would find meaning and purpose giving joy and comfort to those she loved and being part of a community made up of family and life-long friends. At the end she would look back on a life well lived.

Our dreams and what it means to live with meaning and

purpose differ widely. But whatever a life well lived means, suffering and tragedy can steal our dreams and our sense of meaning and purpose. Then what?

The God Who Is with Us

Tragedy was not the end of Mary's story, and it doesn't need to be the end of ours. When tragedy strikes, we need to remember that we do not face it alone. God is with us in the midst of our suffering. God knows us, loves us, and trusts us.

God knew Mary's name and where she lived. God knew everything about her and loved her. The angel called Mary honored, favored, and blessed. The angel's message may have thrown Mary's life into turmoil but God was with her the whole time.

The greatest pain in suffering can be feeling abandoned and alone. Those who suffer understand they are alone in their pain. No matter how sympathetic or empathetic others are, no matter how many similar circumstances others have faced, suffering people know deeply and instinctively that others don't and can't truly know others' pain. But that doesn't mean we are alone. Mary was never truly alone and neither are we. God was with her. At the very heart of the Christmas stories is *Emmanuel*, God with us. "All this took place to fulfill what had been spoken by the Lord through the prophet: 'Look, the virgin shall conceive and bear a son, and they shall name him Emmanuel,' which means, 'God is with us'" (Matthew 1:22-23).

Christian teaching differs from the world's religions in many ways. But the most striking difference is that God was willing to suffer to save us. Easter, with all of its passion and pain, is the destination of Christmas. Even when other people cannot fathom our pain, God feels it acutely and knows it completely. There is no human tragedy, no suffering, no atrocity, and no disaster that catches God off guard. For the believer this is a great comfort: God knows! God notices! God cares! God is with us!

Jesus said, "God so loved the world that he gave his only Son, so that everyone who believes in him may not perish but may have eternal life. Indeed, God did not send the Son into the world to condemn the world, but in order that the world might be saved through him" (John 3:16-17).

When facing a tragedy, it's easy to believe God is ignoring or punishing us. But God's love is eternal and is not invalidated by the suffering we endure or the pain we feel. God knew the pain Mary would suffer as Jesus' mother (Luke 2:34-35). How can God's favor and love mingle with sorrow and suffering? It is a mystery. But for Mary and for us, God's constant, dependable love is healing in the midst of hardship.

Our natural inclination is to reject suffering and push it away. We cannot see the good it brings or the possibilities it reveals. Suffering is a summons to trust God for opportunities that are beyond our line of sight. God called Mary to the greatest act of parenting in human history. The price tag of that privilege was suffering. Mary accepted the terms of her call and was rewarded with the honor of being Jesus' mother (Luke 1:31-33) and the most celebrated woman in human history.

In tragedy, we learn who we are at the deepest levels. We forge our character in these fires. God knew Mary was the kind of person who could take on a challenge, face tragedy, and faithfully follow him. God trusted her with history's greatest treasure. God was with her. "We also boast in our sufferings, knowing that suffering produces endurance, and endurance produces character, and character produces hope, and hope does not disappoint us, because God's love has been poured into our hearts through the Holy Spirit that has been given to us" (Romans 5:3-5).

Shocked and Confused

Even when we know God is with us, tragedy shocks and confuses us. It doesn't make sense. It seems implausible, incomprehensible, and uncontrollable. Mary said to the angel, "How will this be, since I am a virgin?" (Luke 1:34).

Tragedy often seems implausible, not because these things can't happen but because we believe they won't happen to us. Mary's circumstances defied all logic: a pregnant virgin carrying a divine child? There are many things we think are not supposed to happen, but they still do. Parents should not have to bury their children. Marriages should last a lifetime, unstained by betrayal and adultery. Childhood should be carefree and fun, not a time of starvation, illness, or peril. But horrible, unthinkable events happen every day.

Suffering often seems incomprehensible. It leaves us dazed and disoriented. We feel like pieces of driftwood, bobbing on a stormy sea. We can't figure out where the riptides are taking us and it's terrifying. We search for glimmers of good, but everything seems dark. Finding meaning in pain calms our souls and makes coping easier. At least it seems that way. In times of suffering our soul screams, "This can't be happening!" We want to wake up and realize it was all just a nightmare.

Suffering often seems uncontrollable. When Mary said yes to God, it set off an unstoppable chain reaction. During the next nine months, pregnancy dominated every aspect of her life. The child grew in her womb while her body changed, her hormones surged, and her belly swelled. She was not in control of these things. We cannot control our suffering either.

Sudden and unexpected events are like an earthquake that shatters the safe lives we thought we built on bedrock. We want to rebuild and repair but we are afraid to make plans or decisions. We grind through each day, hoping that somehow things will turn out all right. Uncertainty is a heavy burden to carry. "Beloved, do not be surprised at the fiery ordeal that is taking place among you to test you, as though something strange were happening to you. But rejoice insofar as you are sharing Christ's sufferings, so that you may also be glad and shout for joy when his glory is revealed" (1 Peter 4:12-13).

The Arrival of Fear

Fear and uncertainty storm into our lives with tragedy. The prospect of being pregnant and unmarried must have been terrifying for Mary. Like her, we struggle with the angel's command: "Fear not!"

We fear because we do not trust what our eyes cannot see. We look at things with our limited perspective in a changing and uncertain world. We forget to view our challenges in the light of a sovereign, loving, wise, and powerful God. We fail to take into account God's eternally trustworthy character. God can be trusted.

We fear because we don't know and can't understand God's greater plan. God's love, compassion, and concern are not part of our calculations. We only see what is, not what can be. God alone knows the good and glorious future that awaits those who follow him. God has a plan.

We fear because we want what we want. We do not always want the plan God is working out in us. We think we know better. The idea that we are better off not getting what we want is inconceivable. It's even more inconceivable that getting what we do not want, what is painful or difficult, is really our greatest good. We'd rather God be part of our plans than us be part of his.

We fear because we want control. Something deep within us

recoils from knowing our lives are in another's control. We resist the idea that our hopes and aspirations are not the greatest and most important good in the universe. We reject the notion that we might be asked to sacrifice and suffer.

What we don't realize is that God knows all about our fears. God uses the uncertainty in our lives for transformation. God catches our attention when we loosen our grip on the things and people we cling to. God is at work in circumstance, coincidence, and serendipity. God's plan doesn't need our permission or even our cooperation.

With God, things aren't falling apart. They are falling into place.

The Right Heart

Mary had a choice. Would she believe the angel's message? Would she accept this assignment? Mary's answer was decisive and clear. Yes. (In this way, of course, we can see some similarities and some differences between Mary and Zechariah. Both are faced with the question of whom and what to believe. Probably each of us has had Zechariah moments and each of us Mary moments—moments where it is hard to believe, and moments where our assent to the inexplicable and even confusing work of God in our lives is immediate and decisive.)

"Here am I, the servant of the Lord; let it be with me according to your word" (Luke 1:38). Mary could have refused the angel's offer. The Bible is full of stories of people who had equally dramatic encounters with God and refused to be part of God's work in the world. The most dramatic example is the first. Adam and Eve lived in an idyllic world and walked with God in perfect intimacy (Genesis 3). When tempted, they chose disobedience. They said no to God and that changed everything. People have been saying no to God ever since.

Mary had good reasons to say no. The pregnancy would destroy her relationship with Joseph, her reputation, and her life. The only way to keep the life she cherished was to say no to the angel.

It was a crucial decision. Nothing indicates that the angel was forceful or coercive. All we know is that Gabriel brought God's message and Mary said yes. Many who face life-changing circumstances feel they don't have a choice. Having no choice or say in the situation is what makes it tragic. No one chooses suffering, but everyone chooses a response.

Mary's response demonstrated three things about her character and relationship with God.

"Here am I, the servant of the Lord" (Luke 1:38a). First, Mary did not insist on controlling her own destiny. The foundation of her relationship with God was service. There is no bargaining or quid pro quo in Mary's answer. She knew who she was and was secure in her relationship with God. She did not say yes out of weakness, insecurity, or gullibility. Despite her youth, Mary was wise enough to completely give herself to God and his great cause. It's an example worth following. Do we exist to serve or be served? Do we live for our own ends or give ourselves to greater things?

"Let it be with me according to your word" (Luke 1:38b). Second, Mary submitted to God's will. In our world, submission is disdained as weakness. But Mary's submission wasn't weak. It was a muscular submission that accepts the consequences. She couldn't have known everything that awaited her in the future, but she gave herself to God anyway. That's courageous and incredibly strong.

Mary trusted the angel and the God who sent him. She knew the risks that came with her decision but believed she was safe in God's hands. Trust is a rare and precious commodity. Most people trust others slowly, one drop at a time, carefully, and within clearly defined limits. Even the people closest to us are capable of inflicting incredible pain. Trust is a struggle for most of us because we aren't very trustworthy either.

Mary's God is ultimately and always trustworthy. She trusted God with everything, including her body, her baby, and her future. God is powerful and able to do what is promised. God is all wise and never mistaken. God knew better than Mary what was best for her. When life was difficult, God made a way for her.

For most people, the thought of total trust even in God is beyond comprehension. But those who trust God find great comfort and peace. Generation after generation, Christians have submitted to God's call and surrendered their lives, their wills, and their dreams, just like Mary, and learned this lesson. Even in tragedy, those who trust God discover they are his beloved children. They know God is with them. He is Emmanuel.

The Rest of the Story

The angel's visit seemed to smash Mary's life to pieces. But we know the rest of her story. Joseph stood by her side in marriage and parenthood (Matthew 1:24-25). Their baby Jesus was born in Bethlehem while they were traveling for a Roman census (Luke 2:4-7). Angels, shepherds, and the magi celebrated his birth (Matthew 2:2). When news of a newborn Messiah reached King Herod, he became jealous and wanted to kill the baby (Matthew 2:16-18). Warned by an angel in a dream, Mary and Joseph fled to Egypt and lived as refugees until it was safe to return to Nazareth with their miracle child (Matthew 2:13-15, 19-22). Eventually, they had other sons and daughters (Matthew 12:46; John 7:1-5; Acts 1:14) and spent decades in their hometown with their extended families. On the surface, Mary's life didn't look very different from the one she imagined before the angel.

And yet everything was different. Mary's life was immeasurably richer and fuller as the mother of the Messiah. She participated in the fulfillment of ancient prophecies and God's magnificent kingdom work on earth. She lived with Jesus in her home and watched him grow and learn for thirty years. Mary witnessed

Jesus' first miracle, turning water into wine at a wedding celebration (John 2:1-11). Mary was proud of her son as he became respected as a great rabbi and miracle healer.

But not everything went well. Her four other boys—James, Joseph, Simon, and Judas (Matthew 13:55)—didn't believe (John 5:7), thought Jesus was insane (Mark 3:31-35), and went to Capernaum to collect him. When Jesus preached in Nazareth, his own people turned against him and wanted to kill him for blasphemy (Luke 4:16-29). His popularity and opposition both grew over three years until Jesus was arrested in Jerusalem. Mary watched God's salvation mission with a front-row perspective, from the dark hour of her son's crucifixion (John 19:25-27), to the surprise of the Resurrection (Mark 16:1), and promise of his ascension (Acts 1:11). This ordinary woman who led an extraordinary life is admired and honored more than two thousand years later.

No one would envy Mary's life. No one would want the pain and suffering she endured. She had to deal with great challenges and her life was sometimes in danger. But no life is measured only by its challenges. Life is best measured by how well the challenges are met.

Something Great to Do

Mary did great things with her life in the midst of hardship. She was called to carry and nurture in her own body Jesus, who was fully God and fully man. Mary nurtured Jesus in her womb, at her breast, and in her home as he grew from child to man. Then she released Jesus to the world, future generations, and all of us. Mary gave the greatest Christmas gift ever given—the redeemer of all mankind. Jesus' life, death, and resurrection divided history and opened the doors of heaven.

When faced with tragedy, many people lose sight of the great good that can result. They lament what they would have done if only things had been different. In a way, all who suffer undergo a transformation. We are pregnant with pain; we nurture it, and ultimately deliver what grows in us to the world. Bitterness, hatred, and cruelty can grow in the soil of suffering. Much of the pain in our world is passed from generation to generation. The seeds of future horror are sown in misery, watered with hate, and inevitably produce poisoned fruit. It doesn't have to be this way.

Injury does not require retribution. Bitterness is not automatic. There is no law demanding the injured to reciprocate and no requirement that they nurture animosity. Suffering makes hate possible but not inevitable. The crop that grows from our wounds can be beautiful and beneficial or hate-filled and harmful, depending on what we decide to cultivate in our hearts.

A Challenging Choice

Those who suffer choose what grows in their lives. They can plant their suffering in the soil of forgiveness, water it with grace, and grow the fruit of hope. The crop they harvest blesses and doesn't curse, builds and doesn't destroy. This is the mark of great men and women—they invest in a legacy that spreads hope and changes lives.

People can choose forgiveness or revenge, to look back or look forward, to build up or tear down. They can lament what has been lost or celebrate what is yet to come. In every great tragedy there is potential for great good. We choose what we make of our suffering and what our suffering makes of us.

Like Mary, we have something great to do. Our call is to nurture the grace and beauty of our loving God and display it to the world. That capacity is in us because we are made in God's image. But we must consciously choose to infuse our lives with divine love, mercy, and patience.

Like Mary, we have access to a power beyond our own. Mary turned to God, the ultimate source of grace and reconciliation. God gave her the strength and courage she needed to forgive. We must do the same.

The Bible tells us, Mary "treasured all these things in her heart" (Luke 2:51). These ponderings included the suffering, humiliation, and pain of her unexpected and miraculous pregnancy. The treasure was that God was with her in her suffering. She could deal with her pain because she knew God loved and sustained her. God was at work in her life. That is a treasure worth keeping.

Like Mary, we have something great to do with our lives. It is to experience the miraculous alchemy that transforms suffering into beauty, forgiveness, strength, and love. It's what we need. It's what our world needs.

The road of bitterness has mile markers of denial, bargaining, anger, despair, resentment, and devastation. People remain in mourning for the rest of their days. Reality is only a consolation prize for the lives they lost. Bitterness is a well-worn path and easy to follow. But it only leads to more misery.

Mary chose the road that made her better. She found strength and encouragement that helped her stay on the narrow path. The strength Mary found was divine.

> In those days Mary set out and went with haste to a Judean town in the hill country, where she entered the house of Zechariah and greeted Elizabeth. When Elizabeth heard Mary's greeting, the child leaped in her womb. And Elizabeth was filled with the Holy Spirit and exclaimed with a loud cry, "Blessed are you among women, and blessed is the fruit of your womb. And why has this happened to me, that the mother of my Lord comes to me? For as soon as I heard the sound of your greeting, the child in my womb leaped for joy. And blessed is she who believed that there would be a fulfillment of what was spoken to her by the Lord." (Luke 1:39-45)

A Song of Praise

Mary visited her cousin Elizabeth to see if the angel's words about her were true. Perhaps Mary needed comfort and guidance from the older woman. Elizabeth had faced her own great challenges and surprises. Perhaps Mary was afraid to go home. Elizabeth's exuberant greeting put her fears to rest. Like the angel, her cousin told Mary she was blessed and so was her baby. It was just the confirmation and encouragement Mary needed.

Mary spontaneously burst into a glorious exultation of praise known as the Magnificat.

> And Mary said,
> "My soul magnifies the Lord,
>   and my spirit rejoices in God my Savior,
> for he has looked with favor on the lowliness of his
>   servant.
>   Surely, from now on all generations will call me
>   blessed;
> for the Mighty One has done great things for me,
>   and holy is his name.
> His mercy is for those who fear him
>   from generation to generation.
> He has shown strength with his arm;
>   he has scattered the proud in the thoughts of their
>   hearts.

> He has brought down the powerful from their thrones,
>> and lifted up the lowly;
> he has filled the hungry with good things,
>> and sent the rich away empty.
> He has helped his servant Israel,
>> in remembrance of his mercy,
> according to the promise he made to our ancestors,
>> to Abraham and to his descendants forever."
> And Mary remained with her about three months and then
> returned to her home. (Luke 1:46-56)

Where did Mary's majestic words come from? Did she compose them on her way to Elizabeth's house? Did she learn them from a wise teacher and recite them with each weary step through the Judean hills? Whatever their source, they are a window into Mary's soul. When all she hoped for seemed swept away, she found strength in God.

We face the same dilemma. There comes a time when those who suffer find the reservoir of human strength is dry. The support of well-meaning friends crumbles. Even those we love can't journey any further with us and there is nowhere else to go. We feel alone. But we aren't. At the end of human efforts, God waits with divine strength.

Mary began to see her circumstances in a new light (Luke 1:46-49). God had not singled her out for punishment. She was destined for history's greatest blessing. Her situation was cause for celebration, not a disaster. So she rejoiced in God's goodness and provision.

Accepting our new reality is essential if we are to survive and ultimately thrive after a tragedy. Softened by the white heat of pain and hammered by circumstance on the anvil of suffering we forge a new shape for our lives. It's never easy. The future we cherished is gone. But in that moment we can find the strength, wisdom, and courage to live better lives. Like iron in the smith's forge, we lose the shape of the old life and a beautiful new creation emerges.

Facing the Future

After three months with Elizabeth, Mary went home to Nazareth (Luke 1:56). We don't know when the angel visited Joseph in the dream or how her family and neighbors responded to her pregnancy.

But Mary faced her new circumstances with courage, grace, and dignity. Mary fulfilled her destiny and persevered until all the angel's promises came true. Thirty-three years after her divine son was born, Mary stood at the foot of the cross. In gratitude for his mother's devotion, Jesus entrusted her to his beloved disciple John (John 19:26-27). She was in the upper room on Pentecost with the disciples and her other sons when the Holy Spirit came (Acts 1:13-14). Mary witnessed the indelible impact that her son Jesus and Elizabeth's son, John, made on the world. Two divinely ordained pregnancies changed everything.

As far as we know Mary lived her final years quietly as the good news of the gospel exploded throughout the known world. The rest of her life may have been commonplace except for news of the apostles' miracles and adventures. She began her incredible journey as an ordinary girl and finished it as an amazing woman.

The day will come when tragedy and suffering pass. We look back at what it did to us and at the way we dealt with the grief and pain. We take stock of who we were and what we did. We face the truth that our present isn't the result of the tragedy alone, but the result of what we chose in our times of suffering.

The ability to bounce back, to regain balance, and to try again is called resilience. When God is with you and sustains you in a dark time, you learn to look for the divine hand the next time trouble comes. You trust more, pray more, and notice more in hardship than you expected to. Your experiences of hope gather and form a web of resilience. Instead of snapping under pressure, you learn to bend, to wait, to trust. You learn that all things are working together for good (Romans 8:28). Maybe not right now, maybe not during your lifetime, but God is doing something in the tragedy that is bigger than you can imagine.

The inevitable questions come: Would you do it all again? Would you change anything if you could? Do you have any regrets? No one ultimately controls what happens in life. We aren't that powerful. But we can live a life of integrity and be proud of the choices we make when life is at its worst. Everyone would like to live his or her best possible life. Not many do.

The question that Mary's story poses to us, each and every Christmas, is, when we face shocking news, potentially tragic news, news that seems to derail—or in fact *does* derail all our plans—will we move toward resilience? Will we listen for, and hear, the Holy that is somehow present in the midst of tragedy? Will we discern the word of God that has come to us, and give ourselves over, not to the tragic interpretation, but to that Word? Will we allow that word to grow within us, and allow the Word of grace, not the word of tragedy, to shape our course?

Questions

1. What do you find most comforting in times of sorrow?

2. In your experience what does a person have to do to end mourning and move on in life?

3. What responsibilities do we have to others facing sorrow?

4. Entering another person's sorrow and helping him or her through can be very difficult. Why?

5. In times of sorrow did you find comfort in God's presence? In what ways?

6. What did you learn when you turned to God in times of suffering and tragedy?

7. We don't always find God's comfort and healing when we suffer. What are the results of that unresolved grief, anger, and pain?

8. It's possible pain, anger, and grief linger years after we suffered through a difficult circumstance. If that's the case, what are some things we may need to do?

9. Sometimes our grief is associated with another person and something he or she did to those we love or to us. Is it possible to find comfort and healing without forgiving that person? If not, why not?

Christmas 1968

The year 1968 was a crazy year of contrasts—horrific war and peace treaties, free love and open hate, peaceful demonstrations and violent riots. That year was a memorable one for me, too. I was on the varsity swim team and played in the marching band. I got my driver's license, a secondhand car, my first girlfriend, and my first real job. People told me high school was the best time of my life. I hoped that wasn't true.

But none of that mattered. The year wasn't over, and it kept the worst for last.

The days before Christmas were hectic for my older sister Linda, her husband, Ron, and their six-month-old daughter, Wendy. Ron worked at an appliance store where he was a natural salesman—affable, funny, and at ease with everyone. I'd known Ron my entire life and admired him greatly. My whole family loved him.

On Saturday, December 21, 1968, after selling a refrigerator to an elderly couple, Ron turned to wave good-bye and suddenly felt very sick. Overwhelmed by nausea and an excruciating head-ache, he told his boss he was sick and headed home. When Ron got there, he told Linda he might have the flu and went to lie down.

A few hours later, Linda went into their darkened bedroom to see if Ron needed anything. She found him unresponsive and comatose. An ambulance rushed Ron to the local hospital for tests, and then transferred him to the regional medical center for more examinations. But it wasn't the flu. It was a massive cerebral hemorrhage. A weakened blood vessel ruptured deep in his brain. The best neurosurgeons at one of the nation's finest hospitals did everything they could to save him. They couldn't. My family kept vigil in his room for almost a week, but Ron never woke up. He died at age twenty-seven on December 26.

Christmas 1968 took away more than it gave. Linda lost her husband, the love of her life. Little Wendy lost her dad before she could even remember him. I lost the coolest brother-in-law I could ever hope to have.

On the day of the funeral, the sanctuary was overflowing with mourners. Linda held Wendy in her lap, flanked by our family and Ron's family in the front rows. I sat in the choir loft as a member of the choir. At the end of the service, hundreds of people streamed past the coffin and paused to show respect. They turned to my sister Linda, shook her hand or hugged her neck, and made their way sobbing from the church.

When the last mourner walked down the center aisle and the organist finished playing funeral music, the choir stood and processed into the practice room. As I pulled off my cowl and robe, another choir member put his hand on my shoulder and asked if I was all right.

They all thought it was grief and sadness. It wasn't. I felt rage, overwhelming white-hot rage at a God who would make my niece an orphan and my sister a widow. I felt rage at the church that taught me to obey any God who let this tragedy happen. Where was God when we needed him the most? God was AWOL, absent without leave. God was not there for Ron in the ICU room, not there for my family in the church. God turned a deaf ear to our prayers and abandoned us at Christmas. I was done with that kind of God. Done.

CHAPTER 3

WHY HAS THIS HAPPENED TO ME?

Elizabeth's Journey from Unfairness to Gratitude

It's Not Fair

Why can't life be fair? Why do bad things happen? In every generation and culture, people have tried to understand the nature of fairness. We don't know why some people are prosperous and secure while others are impoverished and endangered. We don't know why a tornado hits one house and not another. We can't prevent life-altering accidents, incidences, or diseases. Life is not fair, never has been, and never will be. But we wish it were.

Personal decisions, attitudes, and actions make life more painful than it needs to be. Governments, societies, families disappoint and inflict pain. Natural disasters happen. True enough. Sometimes people suffer for no reason at all. There is no one and nothing to blame and no explanation for our misery. Unfairness is part of a very painful package called life.

We wish we could fix what's wrong with the world. We are horrified by atrocities and tragedies across the world and in our own neighborhoods. We are outraged when our loved ones are mistreated or abused. We are angry when something unfair and unexpected happens to us. We see inequality on the playground, at our jobs, in the union meeting, and in the halls of government. Sometimes laws are passed, speeches given, sacrifices made, and wars fought to make the world a fairer and better place. But unfairness and injustice are still as persistent and predictable as the sun rising in the east.

Luke introduces us to Elizabeth, the mother of John the Baptist. She is dealing with the unfair burden of infertility.

In the days of King Herod of Judea, there was a priest named Zechariah, who belonged to the priestly order of Abijah. His wife was a descendant of Aaron, and her name was Elizabeth. Both of them were righteous before God, living blamelessly according to all the commandments and regulations of the Lord. But they had no children, because Elizabeth was barren, and both were getting on in years. Once when [Zechariah] was serving as priest before God and his section was on duty, he was chosen by lot, according to the custom of the priesthood, to enter the sanctuary of the Lord and offer incense. Now at the time of the incense offering, the whole assembly of the people was praying outside. Then there appeared to him an angel of the Lord, standing at the right side of the altar of incense. When Zechariah saw him, he was terrified; and fear overwhelmed him. But the angel said to him, "Do not be afraid, Zechariah, for your prayer has been heard. Your wife Elizabeth will bear you a son, and you will name him John. You will have joy and gladness, and many will rejoice at his birth, for he will be great in the sight of the Lord."...Zechariah said to the angel, "How will I know that this is so? For I am an old man, and my wife is getting on in years." The angel replied, "I am Gabriel. I stand in the presence of God, and I have been sent to speak to you and to bring you this good news. But now, because you did not believe my words, which will be fulfilled in their time, you will become mute, unable to speak, until the day these things occur."

Meanwhile the people were waiting for Zechariah, and wondered at his delay in the sanctuary. When he did come out, he could not speak to them, and they realized that he had seen a vision in the sanctuary. He kept motioning to them and remained unable to speak. When his time of service was ended, he went to his home.

After those days his wife Elizabeth conceived, and for five months she remained in seclusion. She said, "This is what the Lord has done for me when he looked favorably

on me and took away the disgrace I have endured among
my people." (Luke 1:5-14, 18-25)

A little later in the narrative, Mary visited Elizabeth's home
(Luke 1:41-43). Upon seeing Mary, Elizabeth questions, "Why
has this happened to me?" (v. 43 CEB). In the context of Elizabeth's greeting, the question is positive—it is a blessing and
pleasant surprise to see Mary. But the question "Why has this
happened to me?" can also be negative—why do bad things happen? Why is life unfair? Prior to Zechariah's angelic visit in the
temple, Elizabeth must have also asked, "Why has this happened
to me?" about her barrenness.

Fairness and Justice

Fairness and justice are not synonyms. Justice means people
get what they deserve or what society demands. Justice holds
people accountable for their actions and rewards or punishes
accordingly. Society, the family, and employers have standards
for which behaviors are acceptable. Justice maintains those standards and issues punishment when behavior is unacceptable and
rewards when standards are met.

Fairness is different. Fairness is more fundamental and objec-
tive. Fairness demands that everyone play by the same rules and
that the playing field is level. For instance, the handicap system in
golf enables golfers of all skill levels to compete on an equitable

basis. The distance from tee to hole on a golf course is adjusted to accommodate men, women, and youth. Golf has a lot of rules and guidelines to make it fair and enjoyable for everyone.

Some societies and governments strive to make life as fair as possible. They enforce equal access and affirmative action laws to reduce discrimination. They adhere to building codes that allow accessibility regardless of physical handicap. They have regulatory agencies, watchdog groups, and consumer advocates to monitor the safety and quality of goods and services. But fairness is not always the norm. In every corner of the world there are people who are treated differently because of karma, religion, nationality, gender, race, caste, or tribe.

The world is not fair. Justice is not universal. Some suffer terrible accidents or diseases while others grow healthy and strong. Some people are born with high intelligence and able bodies while others are born with mental impairments and physical deformities. We don't know why. Life isn't fair.

The Curious Case of Elizabeth: Before the Angel

Elizabeth experienced both sides of the fairness question. She was both victim and victor, cursed and blessed, sufferer and survivor. Her experience with unfair suffering and miraculous good fortune can be divided into two distinct periods: before and after the angel's visit.

Elizabeth was childless in a time and culture that measured a woman's value by her fertility. Barrenness was a disgrace and a sign of God's disfavor. It was always the woman's fault and was grounds for divorce because having an heir was imperative. Elizabeth didn't deserve barrenness. It wasn't fair.

The Bible is clear. She and Zechariah were "righteous before God, living blamelessly according to all the commandments and regulations of the Lord" (Luke 1:6). The Old Testament Scriptures consistently equated obedience with fertility, productivity, and blessing. Elizabeth's infertility seems not only unfair, but unjust as well. There was an apparent discrepancy between what God promised and what God delivered.

> If you heed these ordinances, by diligently observing them, the Lord your God will maintain with you the covenant loyalty that he swore to your ancestors; he will love you, bless you, and multiply you; he will bless the fruit of your womb and the fruit of your ground, your grain and your wine and your oil, the increase of your cattle and the issue of your flock, in the land that he swore to your ancestors to give you. You shall be the most blessed of peoples, with neither sterility nor barrenness among you or your livestock. (Deuteronomy 7:12-14)

Zechariah and Elizabeth were steeped in the beliefs and traditions of their people. Their understanding of the situation centered on one belief: God controls human fertility. Children are from the Lord, a reward and blessing. A man with many children can be proud. Those without children were not blessed and had every reason to feel ashamed.

> Sons are indeed a heritage from the LORD,
>> the fruit of the womb a reward.
> Like arrows in the hand of a warrior
>> are the sons of one's youth.
> Happy is the man who has
>> his quiver full of them.
> He shall not be put to shame
>> when he speaks with his enemies in the gate.
> (Psalm 127:3-5)

Elizabeth felt the disgrace. Perhaps her heart ached every time she heard of another pregnancy in the village or the cries of joy when a baby was born. She may have cringed when young parents showed off their newborns or saw young children at play. Every mother trailing a toddler through the dusty streets reminded her of the unfairness of her barren life.

It wasn't any better for Zechariah. How many times had the men of the village slapped one another on the back at the news of a coming child? How many times had he circumcised another man's son? How many boys had he taught the Torah and watched grow into manhood?

It must have seemed that God had abandoned them. Perhaps there were periods of significant soul-searching, trying to understand why God ignored their plight and their prayers. It's one thing to think you're the victim of bad luck, happenstance, or evil. It's quite another to believe you've been singled out by the almighty Creator of the universe for punishment and live every day under his angry glare.

Perhaps they didn't blame God. Maybe they blamed each other. Did each spouse wonder what hidden sin in the other brought God's wrath down on them?

More likely they blamed themselves. But the majority of that burden fell on Elizabeth, who longed to give her husband a son. It is a testimony to their deep and abiding love that their marriage survived into old age and Zechariah didn't take another wife.

None of it was true. God wasn't punishing them, hadn't failed them, and hadn't abandoned them. God had a different plan and a different timetable. It wasn't Zechariah's fault or Elizabeth's fault. It wasn't a fault, misfortune, or even bad luck. It just wasn't what they expected or wanted.

By human standards, Zechariah and Elizabeth had good reason to complain, grow bitter, or be angry with God. They had lived well. Other, less-deserving couples had been given children while they remained childless. But their situation couldn't rightly be judged by any human standard.

Zechariah's encounter with Gabriel (Luke 1:5-6) was a

watershed moment that radically altered the course of his life and dramatically impacted everyone in it.

After the Angel

Elizabeth's story does not end in pain and deprivation. It ends in joy and delight. God intervened. Their faith was rewarded. Against all odds and despite the obvious reality of their lives, Elizabeth became pregnant (Luke 1:24-25).

Elizabeth's blessings were no fairer than her sufferings. No other barren woman got the miraculous restoration of her fertility through an angelic visit. Unfairness isn't found only in struggle or pain. Blessings and joys blithely accepted as if deserved are also unfair. Why are some tear-stained prayers to the heavens answered, and others not?

People living in comfort enjoy the blessings they have and give little thought to others who suffer. They accept their privileged state as an entitlement they deserve.

Meanwhile, people living in poverty and suffering wonder why their misfortune means their children starve and endure preventable diseases. Neither deserves their lot.

The Harvest

People treated unfairly sometimes turn their feelings outward with anger, bitterness, jealousy, and hatred. Others turn their feelings inward—and the feelings wind up being self-destructive. You have probably known people who have made this choice—the unfairness they have suffered becomes a self-perpetuating bitterness. They limp through life and relationships hamstrung by suffering.

Fermented pain begets crime, conflict, and cruelty. Fingers point toward the government, the wealthy, the powerful, anyone to blame. When that proves futile, people turn on anyone who has the misfortune of being close. Families perpetrate verbal abuse, cruelty, and punishment. Neighborhoods self-implode with arson, theft, rape, and murder. In the end it is a very bitter harvest for everyone.

Elizabeth chose another way. She refused the poison of anger, despair, and doubt. The secret lay in the faith that sustained her hope and gave meaning to her pain. Her steadfastness led to a happy life and a miracle.

What happens to us in life matters. But what matters more is what we do with what happens. Wealth can be hoarded or shared. Power can be used to abuse or protect. Influence can be used to corrupt or inspire. Our response to the circumstances of life depends on the mental, emotional, moral, psychological, and spiritual paradigms we apply.

Zechariah and Elizabeth were first-century Jews descended from the people of the Exodus. Their God heard cries for help and delivered people in times of trial. They trusted God's

77

power, goodness, and wisdom, even when God's ways were mysterious. As the descendants of priests, Zechariah and Elizabeth knew what the Psalms and Prophets said about God.

First, they believed in God's power. Beginning with the Genesis stories of creation and Exodus stories of deliverance, the God of the Israelites was mighty and powerful. Their situation may have seemed hopeless and they may have felt helpless. But God had delivered their ancestors from Egyptian slavery, sustained them in the wilderness, and led them to the Promised Land. God could and would deliver them. Even in dark times, they offered praise and gratitude to God.

Second, they believed in God's wisdom. They knew countless stories of people who faced impossible circumstances, like young David taking on the giant Goliath. In those unfair and unlikely situations, God displayed greater wisdom beyond what human eyes could see. Even when the Israelites were captured and exiled to faraway countries, God had a plan for restoration. Zechariah and Elizabeth believed that God was at work for their good, even when things looked bad and the road got hard.

> Bless our God, O peoples,
>> let the sound of his praise be heard,
> who has kept us among the living,
>> and has not let our feet slip.
> For you, O God, have tested us;

> you have tried us as silver is tried.
> You brought us into the net;
>   you laid burdens on our backs;
> you let people ride over our heads;
>   we went through fire and through water;
> yet you have brought us out to a spacious place.
> (Psalm 66:8-12)

Third, they believed in God's goodness. Zechariah and Elizabeth's childless marriage was heartbreaking. But the rock-solid foundation of their faith secured them to a loving God who could redeem the worst of situations. Their faith gave them the strength to live with confidence in the face of great disappointment, personal pain, and injustice.

Fourth, they believed in God's justice. It was woven into their faith: the unrighteous faced God's judgment and the righteous were vindicated. Zechariah and Elizabeth trusted God's justice. It wasn't easy, but they looked beyond their plight with the eyes of faith and grasped a deeper and truer reality.

> Seek the Lord while he may be found,
>   call upon him while he is near;
> let the wicked forsake their way,
>   and the unrighteous their thoughts;
> let them return to the Lord, that he may have mercy
>   on them,

and to our God, for he will abundantly pardon.
For my thoughts are not your thoughts,
nor are your ways my ways, says the LORD.
For as the heavens are higher than the earth,
so are my ways higher than your ways
and my thoughts than your thoughts.
(Isaiah 55:6-9)

Why does this matter to us today? It matters because Zechariah and Elizabeth lived out of this radically different paradigm. They did not sink into fatalistic despair, and they were not oblivious to or naive about their circumstances. They responded to their pain with courage, to their uncertainty with faith, and to their unfairness with confidence. They were exactly the kind of people God wanted them to be.

Faith on Display

God's great wisdom was so perfectly embodied by Jesus that his words became part of the foundation of morality and justice. He moved beyond the legalism of rabbinic law and spoke of the importance of people's hearts, not just their behaviors. His words are so ingrained in culture that people quote the teachings of Jesus without realizing their divine source.

[Jesus said,] "Love your enemies, do good to those who hate you, bless those who curse you, pray for those who abuse you. If anyone strikes you on the cheek, offer the other also; and from anyone who takes away your coat do not withhold even your shirt. Give to everyone who begs from you; and if anyone takes away your goods, do not ask for them again. Do to others as you would have them do to you." (Luke 6:27-31)

God's goodness was on display in Christ's gentle way with children, his willingness to touch the physically infirm, his love for the outcasts of society, and his commissioning of everyday people to become disciples (Luke 8:1-3). The religious leaders and teachers of the law could not understand Jesus' love and affection for broken people.

And as [Jesus] sat at dinner in the house, many tax collectors and sinners came and were sitting with him and his disciples. When the Pharisees saw this, they said to his disciples, "Why does your teacher eat with tax collectors and sinners?" But when he heard this, he said, "Those who are well have no need of a physician, but those who are sick. Go and learn what this means, 'I desire mercy, not sacrifice.' For I have come to call not the righteous but sinners." (Matthew 9:10-13)

God's justice was seen in Jesus' reversal of cultural norms. Jesus fiercely condemned the self-satisfied religious people who thought they were righteous and good. He criticized the people who concerned themselves only with outward appearances and shallow morality. Jesus said, "Woe to you, scribes and Pharisees, hypocrites! For you are like whitewashed tombs, which on the outside look beautiful, but inside they are full of the bones of the dead and of all kinds of filth. So you also on the outside look righteous to others, but inside you are full of hypocrisy and lawlessness" (Matthew 23:27-28).

God's mercy was seen in Jesus' unconditional love. Jesus loved the lepers, paralytics, demon-possessed, and prostitutes by healing their bodies, minds, and spirits (Luke 5:13, 20; 6:18; 7:48). He accepted foreigners, praised unbelievers, socialized with women, and defied political leaders. In Jesus, God's loving-kindness was visible in the transformation of people's lives: the blind saw, the deaf heard, the lame walked, and the dead came back to life.

Finally, God's rescue plan for humanity was revealed in Jesus. The God who delivered the Israelites had an even bigger mission in mind. Jesus made salvation available to everyone who believed. "Jesus said to them, 'Truly I tell you, the tax collectors and the prostitutes are going into the kingdom of God ahead of you.'...When the chief priests and the Pharisees heard his parables, they realized that he was speaking about them. They wanted to arrest him, but they feared the crowds, because they regarded him as a prophet" (Matthew 21:31b, 45-46).

Jesus' teachings are just as radical today. We are accustomed to proving theories and solving mysteries with facts, figures, and evidence. It can be hard to believe in what we can't see. But suppose there is a God who is just, powerful, wise, and trustworthy. Suppose this God really loves us and cares about us and wants to be with us. If that's true, then everything changes.

Before the angel's visit, Elizabeth and Zechariah experienced incredible unfairness and pain. They felt the ache of childlessness. They grieved their diminishing options as time marched on. But their faith set them apart from the rest. They trusted in the wisdom, power, and goodness of God even when they were denied the opportunity to become parents.

> The angel said to [Mary], . . . "And now, your relative Elizabeth in her old age has also conceived a son; and this is the sixth month for her who was said to be barren. For nothing will be impossible with God." Then Mary said, "Here am I, the servant of the Lord; let it be with me according to your word." Then the angel departed from her.
>
> In those days Mary set out and went with haste to a Judean town in the hill country, where she entered the house of Zechariah and greeted Elizabeth. When Elizabeth heard Mary's greeting, the child leaped in her womb. And Elizabeth was filled with the Holy Spirit and exclaimed with a loud cry, "Blessed are you among women, and blessed is the fruit of your womb. And why has this happened to me that the mother of my Lord comes to me? For as soon as I heard

the sound of your greeting, the child in my womb leaped for joy. And blessed is she who believed that there would be a fulfillment of what was spoken to her by the Lord." (Luke 1:35-37, 39-45 CEB)

Count Your Blessings

When Mary came to visit, Elizabeth counted her blessings (Luke 1:39-45). Her question, "Why has this happened to me?" now comes from a place of gratitude. Elizabeth and Mary were blessed that their prayers were heard by God, blessed to participate in God's plan for redemption, and blessed to have an opportunity to encourage one another. Like Elizabeth, we can count our blessings and express our gratitude to God.

First, Elizabeth had the blessing of answered prayer. A child was the one thing that could end her lifelong disappointment. She and Zechariah prayed and waited patiently. It seemed God ignored their cries until that day in the temple. The first time she had morning sickness she knew for sure: God had intervened. The same is true for us. God responds to our greatest needs and deepest pleas, but they're probably not what we had in mind. God acts in our best interest in wonderful ways, but we don't dictate the timetable. Even when we don't like or understand it, God's plan is perfect.

Second, Elizabeth had the blessing of exoneration. With each passing day of her pregnancy, God's grace removed her shame and she never looked back. Sometimes we let failures, mistakes, and tragedies cast long, dark shadows on our lives. A bad decision, a hasty word, or a careless act keep us chained to a heavy anchor of guilt. Elizabeth learned how to release the burdens of the past. Our sins can be erased, and we have a clean slate because Jesus brought redemption at Christmas. Jesus came to give people a life of freedom, forgiveness, and grace.

Third, Elizabeth had the blessing of God's presence. Times of pain and trial can be isolating and overwhelming. But during their years of infertility and shame Elizabeth and Zechariah were not alone. God never leaves us or abandons his creation. It might not be easy to see the divine hand moving in our lives, but God is always there. The greatest joy of the Christmas story is that God came to be with us. Jesus is our Emmanuel, God with us. Always.

Fourth, Elizabeth had the blessing of a heavenly vision. When Mary arrived, Elizabeth felt the presence of God, and her unborn son leaped for joy. Through their two miracle babies, Elizabeth and Mary experienced God in a new and profound way. The greatest longing of the human soul is for God. When God is revealed, we experience deep satisfaction and joy.

Finally, Elizabeth had the blessing of a new life. John's birth changed everything. Elizabeth's priorities, interactions, and routines now revolved around the small, helpless infant who woke her up in the middle of the night. Nothing was ever the same again. Instead of being an old married couple, she and Zechariah were parents. Instead of being quiet, anonymous believers, they were active participants in God's great redemption story. But the biggest change was to their inward condition, not their outward circumstances. They underwent a revolution of perspective, priority, and purpose only God's grace could bring.

Blessing's Purpose

Zechariah's encounter with the angel and Elizabeth's pregnancy were great joys and blessings. But their blessing had a purpose. John was their pride and joy, their hearts' great desire and delight. But their blessing was part of a greater plan and bigger story. Their miracle child became a blessing to the whole world.

> John the baptizer appeared in the wilderness, proclaiming a baptism of repentance for the forgiveness of sins. And people from the whole Judean countryside and all the people of Jerusalem were going out to him, and were baptized by him in the river Jordan, confessing their sins. Now John was clothed with camel's hair, with a leather belt around his waist, and he ate locusts and wild honey. He proclaimed, "The one who is more powerful than I is coming after me; I am not worthy to stoop down and untie the thong of his

sandals. I have baptized you with water; but he will baptize you with the Holy Spirit."

In those days Jesus came from Nazareth of Galilee and was baptized by John in the Jordan. And just as he was coming up out of the water, he saw the heavens torn apart and the Spirit descending like a dove on him. And a voice came from heaven, "You are my Son, the Beloved; with you I am well pleased." (Mark 1:4-11)

When John baptized Jesus in the muddy Jordan River, God spoke from heaven and the Holy Spirit descended like a dove. John was a part of political and religious history as a dissident, protestor, and preacher who called a nation to repentance. John suffered a heartbreaking, awful death as a martyr for his faith.

Herod had arrested John [the Baptist], bound him, and put him in prison on account of Herodias, his brother Philip's wife, because John had been telling him, "It is not lawful for you to have her." Though Herod wanted to put him to death, he feared the crowd, because they regarded him as a prophet. But when Herod's birthday came, the daughter of Herodias danced before the company, and she pleased Herod so much that he promised on oath to grant her whatever she might ask. Prompted by her mother, she said, "Give me the head of John the Baptist here on a platter." The king was grieved, yet out of regard for his oaths and for the guests, he commanded it to be given; he sent and had John beheaded in the prison. The head was brought on a platter and given to the girl, who brought it to her mother. His disciples came and took the body and buried it; then they went and told Jesus.

Now when Jesus heard this, he withdrew from there in a boat to a deserted place by himself. (Matthew 14:3-13)

Elizabeth and Zechariah's answered prayers had very unexpected consequences and a tragic ending. But blessings given by God remain under God's domain. Blessings are not to be squandered on greater comfort, more possessions, or personal pleasures. Blessings are to ultimately give glory to God. So what does God expect from those who are blessed?

First, we recognize and rejoice in the source of blessing. A gracious and generous God gave a miracle child to Zechariah and Elizabeth. John was a gift they didn't earn or deserve and they knew it. Deep gratitude was the only possible response. People can work hard at being good, but none of us truly deserve blessing. We have been given much more than we deserve. Such grace cannot be repaid, but we can respond with joyful gratitude to the Giver of all good things.

Second, we are responsible for our blessings. Zechariah and Elizabeth were entrusted with a child who was a marvelous joy, a miraculous gift, and a magnificent responsibility. John's parents provided for him, loved him, taught him, and cared for him. Blessings are not to be abused, hoarded, neglected, or squandered. The world measures success by what we achieve, acquire, or accumulate, but that is not God's way. When we use our blessings in a way that honors God and serves others, we discover true satisfaction and deep contentment.

Third, we eventually release our blessings. The infant sleeping in Elizabeth's arms grew into a toddler, a boy, and a man. Elizabeth and Zechariah released their blessing as he left home for his prophetic ministry in the wilderness. Sometimes we fear that our gifts will be misused or wasted, but when we are selfish with our blessings they only rot and decay. Letting go sets off a surprising chain reaction as others create new, beautiful things we never could have imagined. Like children, blessings should be held lovingly and lightly—treasured, celebrated, and released to do great and wonderful things in the world.

Fourth, we remain righteous once we have our blessing. When they finally got their heart's desire, Zechariah and Elizabeth continued to live with faithful obedience. They served God with grateful hearts in both adversity and prosperity. Sadly, not everyone manages to steer clear of selfishness and sin when lives are blessed and their prayers are answered. Their blessings become trinkets to squander on small and petty pursuits. They settle for small lives of shallow pleasures and material comfort. They numb themselves from suffering and pain with indulgences and anesthetics. Whatever lessons they might have learned are lost. This kind of life lacks the passion and joy that righteousness and faithfulness bring.

Elizabeth's gratitude was not limited to getting what she wanted. The novelty of motherhood would fade into the reality of childcare with all its struggles and challenges. John did not always bring her happiness. He brought her great pain too. John grew up to be an eccentric wilderness wanderer, a controversial prophet, and a political gadfly. He was a prisoner of conscience and the victim of Herod's drunken, lust-filled promise to a shallow girl and her wicked mother. But John was part of God's greater plan for salvation, and even when it brought her sorrow, Elizabeth was grateful for the blessing of being John's mother.

Why do people experience unfair suffering or receive undeserved blessings? We may never know. But in good times and bad times, we have the assurance that God has a plan beyond what we can see. Accepting our blessings and our trials with equal measures of gratitude frees us from worrying about the question, Why has this happened to me? Remaining faithful as we wait for God's promises will eventually bring tidings of great joy for us, for those we love, and all those we touch.

Will you follow Elizabeth's example and take the journey from unfairness to gratitude?

Questions

1. *What do you think of when you hear the word* fair?

2. *What are the qualities of a "fair" or "just" person? What do you admire about them and their lives?*

3. *Why does feeling that the challenges we face are unfair make them harder to deal with?*

4. *Are there dangers in being too "fair"? If so, what are they?*

5. *What does it take to move from being a victim to overcoming unfairness?*

6. *What is the single greatest challenge to overcoming unfairness and injustice?*

7. *What are your "unfair" blessings? How are you stewarding them?*

8. *Are courage and generosity related? If so, how?*

9. *Are there unhealthy ways of being generous? If so, what are they?*

Christmas 1984

After our daughter and son were born, we wanted to have another child. It didn't happen. Just as we were about to give up hope, we found out she was pregnant.

During the pregnancy, my wife often said that something didn't feel right. She had strange pains and the baby was unusually restless. We figured her body was tired from keeping up with Erika and Paul.

When her water broke, we were excited and thought we'd be home for Christmas. We didn't know she was hemorrhaging until we saw that the fluid was bright, bloody red. Panicked, we rushed to the hospital emergency room as fast as our aging orange Volkswagen Beetle could go.

When the hospital staff finally settled her in her room and attached the fetal monitors, we listened to the steady rhythm of our child's heart. For a moment the crisis seemed over. We breathed a little easier. But it wasn't over, not even close.

The doctor came in. He asked us what happened while examining Linda and watching the monitors. He decided to let nature take its course and walked out the door. We prayed. He took a few steps down the hall, turned around, and came back to examine my wife one more time.

"No. We can't wait. We need to take this baby right now!"

Suddenly the obstetrical and surgical staff jumped into warp speed to prepare Linda for an emergency cesarean section. They handed me scrubs and a surgical mask to put on.

It began: the anesthesia...the scalpel...the incision...the baby.

"Placental abruption," someone said.

"A what?" I asked.

"The placenta pulled away from the wall of the uterus. She's been bleeding into the womb. We don't know if the baby got enough oxygen. The placenta is still partially attached. Oh no, look! The cord was double wrapped and double knotted around the baby's neck. He never could have survived delivery."

"Lucky we didn't let her go," the surgeon muttered to our obstetrician.

Lucky? Is that what the life or death of my wife and child came down to? Luck?

They lifted the baby, limp and blue, cut the cord, and handed him to our pediatrician. I'd heard of blue babies. I figured they'd look like a child shivering in the snow, a little bluish around the lips. No. My son was blue from his head to his feet. He looked dead.

"What's wrong? Where's my baby? Is he OK?" my wife cried.

The pediatrician suctioned the baby's nose and turned him. In a half prayer / half whisper she pleaded, "Breathe, baby. Breathe."

The baby made no response. Nothing. The pediatrician rubbed him, rolled him on his stomach, and patted his back. She rubbed him again more vigorously. She talked to him gently and tried to cajole life into him.

"Breathe, baby. Breathe," she called to him in her soothing, sweet Filipino voice.

Nothing. Absolutely nothing! My heart stopped and sank.

Then suddenly the baby gasped and squalled and squirmed as life erupted from somewhere deep inside. He kicked and flailed at the air, protesting his abrupt removal from the warm, dark womb. With each breath, the cold blue pallor of his skin faded, replaced by new-baby pink.

It was the most beautiful thing I had ever seen!

"He looks good! He's OK," the pediatrician said through her mask. I could see the relief and joy in her eyes. I hoped she could see the gratitude in mine.

They cleaned our son off and swaddled him in a warm blanket. When they finally put Mark in my wife's arms, we cried and laughed and cried again.

We were spared a great agony. I knew it. I just didn't know why. At that moment I didn't really care. I was just glad to be one of the lucky ones.

Christmas morning that year was like no other. I brought Erika and Paul to the hospital to celebrate with their new baby brother and mother. Joy and thanksgiving for the gift of life filled our hearts more than a stack of presents ever would.

I couldn't imagine a better Christmas.

CHAPTER 4

WHAT WILL THIS CHILD BECOME?

The Journey from Control to Creativity

W e like to think we have control of our lives. We think we understand ourselves, and to a point we do. We can offer well-edited versions of our personal histories. We tell the funny anecdotes of our childhood adventures and the sanitized stories of our injuries and accidents, and recall the major events and family milestones like graduations, weddings, births, and deaths. We speak of the people who journey with us—teasing siblings, favorite teachers, doting relatives, loyal friends. Like the current owner of a historical residence, we know there are secret nooks we keep to ourselves, messy closets we conceal from others, and dark basement areas no one dares to enter. Most of the time, we keep our pasts in the past.

As for the present, we know the boundaries of our existence and the people we live beside ... at least we think we do. If we stop to examine more closely, we notice there are forces we cannot understand and patterns we do not recognize. Sometimes we are blind to our weaknesses and overestimate our strengths. But we are suspended in the present moment, unable to fix the mistakes of the past or prevent the missteps of the future. Most of the time, we take the present at face value.

The future is life's great undiscovered territory. The future is invisible to us, though we try to imagine it. Everyone wants to control the future. People make plans, arrive at decisions, and mark their calendars, shaping the future of their dreams. The troubling truth is that no one can control the future. There are too many variables and factors that impact our plans.

The present moment is all we control. The future is vast but it arrives one second at a time. With each passing moment, the size of our future shrinks. Time is an ever-decreasing resource. Sooner or later each person runs out of time. Awful tragedies, cruel diseases, and sudden accidents snuff out many lives sooner than expected. Other people outlive their contemporaries and spend their final years alone. But eventually everyone dies.

When a baby is born, we set aside our pessimism for a while and allow ourselves to dream. A newborn is full of potential and promise, fresh and clean like a new diary whose pages are yet to be filled. That long-awaited day came for Elizabeth and Zechariah to become parents.

Now the time came for Elizabeth to give birth, and she bore a son. Her neighbors and relatives heard that the Lord had shown his great mercy to her, and they rejoiced with her.

On the eighth day they came to circumcise the child, and they were going to name him Zechariah after his father. But his mother said, "No; he is to be called John." They said to her, "None of your relatives has this name." Then they began motioning to his father to find out what name he wanted to give him. He asked for a writing tablet and wrote, "His name is John." And all of them were amazed. Immediately his mouth was opened and his tongue freed, and he began to speak, praising God. Fear came over all their neighbors, and all these things were talked about throughout the entire hill country of Judea. All who heard them pondered them and said, "What then will this child become?" For, indeed, the hand of the Lord was with him. (Luke 1:57-66)

Confronting the Future

Talk about strange! For months, people of the Judean hill country watched the impossible unfold. More precisely, they observed two impossible things: their neighbor Elizabeth's postmenopausal pregnancy and their preacher Zechariah's unexplainable silence.

Things didn't get any less strange after their baby was born. Zechariah and Elizabeth insisted on naming their boy John, going against the convention of their culture and time. Even more incredible was the sudden restoration of Zechariah's voice and his dramatic prophecy. Strange indeed!

The events of the day John was born spread like wildfire through the village. No wonder people were afraid, marveled at his birth, and talked about his future. Zechariah's mysterious encounter in the temple and Elizabeth's miraculous pregnancy pointed toward one conclusion: this child was destined for something special. The neighbors could only imagine and wonder, "What then will this child become?" (Luke 1:66).

It is a profound question. What will happen to this unformed life? What future is yet to be discovered? How will this baby's destiny unfold? Even as adults we look at our unrealized future and ask, "What will I become?" How we answer determines whether we find the happiness and satisfaction we so prize. It matters to other people too. Our humanity connects us, and one individual's fate impacts the happiness and satisfaction of many others. Sometimes the rules of society and the expectations of others leave little room for personal choice. It's easy for things to get off-track.

Some people don't consider the needs of others. They just charge ahead. Their pursuits, pleasures, and pride crowd out every other consideration. They cheat and lie to succeed at work. They commit adultery and recklessly abandon their families. The bright light of their achievements, wealth, and success outshines whatever damage other people suffer.

Other people put themselves very last on their to-do list. They subjugate their own plans to care for others, whether a mother sacrificing for her family, a pastor devoted to his congregation, or a teacher who never has a child of her own. Their sacrificial giving takes its toll as their emotional needs go unmet and their bodies suffer from neglect. Their dreams remain in the dark and never see the light of day.

Somewhere between the extremes of selfishness and selflessness is the responsible stewardship of personal potential. Like any work of art, the hands of the artist create the future. A steady grip on the brush, chisel, or pen allows us to explore the passions of our hearts and the ideas of our minds. We choose the colors and patterns of our canvas, the lines and shapes that form our life's work and legacy. We create a masterpiece that is ours alone. What we create largely determines whether we find meaning and joy in life.

The future is more than a moment that has not yet arrived. It is the life that waits. In each passing moment, the future flows like water through our hands, dripping from the present into the pool of the past. The future depends on what happens to us and how we respond. But getting to the future we want isn't about letting time pass aimlessly.

So what is our future and how do we get there?

The answer depends on how we understand our role in creating the future. In some ways, John was lucky. His future started with an angelic announcement and his birth was heralded by a prophecy from his father, Zechariah.

> "And you, child, will be called the prophet of the Most
> High;
>> for you will go before the Lord to prepare his ways,
> to give knowledge of salvation to his people
>> by the forgiveness of their sins.
> By the tender mercy of our God,
>> the dawn from on high will break upon us,
> to give light to those who sit in darkness and in the
>> shadow of death,
>> to guide our feet into the way of peace."
> The child grew and became strong in spirit, and he was in the wilderness until the day he appeared publicly to Israel. (Luke 1:76-80)

Reality Therapy

Four critical truths about the future are clear from John's story.

First, the future is ours to make. We create with what we have: our culture, genetics, family, and all we inherit in our place in the world. Life has boundaries, but they are much wider, higher, and deeper than we suppose and there is much more space to create life than most realize. We cannot soar like the eagle, but we can build machines that fly. John's calling was to be a prophet, but it was also to become his unique self.

Second, we control how we respond to what happens to us. Much of life is beyond our control. Other people, forces of nature, tides of history, and random events shape us, but we are not powerless. We retain the ability to respond to events that impinge on our future. Each blessing, pain, sorrow, and joy is an opportunity. Every choice nudges our future in one direction or another. Every decision opens some doors and closes others. In the end, we reach a future created by our accumulated responses over time.

Third, our possibilities are limited by cause and effect. Some philosophers and theologians play semantic games with the nature of freedom, choice, and will, but consequences are real and unavoidable. The results of each person's choices ripple through time. It's impossible to know the full implications of every action, but our decisions matter.

The fact that Christmas is celebrated two thousand years after Christ's birth is, from a human perspective, the result of unintended consequences. The religious and political leaders of Christ's day conspired to falsely accuse, arrest, and execute him. They intended to change the future in their favor. They felt threatened by Jesus so they silenced him. They had power, wealth, and status and Jesus did not. Their plan should have worked. It didn't.

Finally, the future doesn't exist yet. It is made from what is possible, not what is predetermined. This gets really tricky depending on your theological beliefs. God is the Creator and Sustainer of the universe. God is at work to bring events to their ultimate conclusion. God is sovereign and has the ability to intervene in any time or place. I couldn't agree more!

There is absolutely no doubt God knows the end from the beginning and everything in between. No one should ever doubt that the creator of the universe guides history and is at work in every circumstance, every happenstance, and every tragedy to bring his plans and purposes to their ultimate conclusion. He can and does intervene in individual lives and nations, in space and time when and how he wishes. That's why we pray.

But people create futures with every action and decision. At the point of decision, when the future is on the line and we have to choose, we function that way. That in no way limits God's power or sovereignty. It proves it. Human freedom exists inside the reality he created and is carried out by beings he made with the capabilities he gave them. God created humanity in the divine image and entrusted us with free will. God equipped us with minds, talents, and capabilities. Our actions and inactions have real consequences. Our choices and decisions shape the path of the future. But God has ultimate and final control.

Creating the Future

Creativity—the ability to imagine something new and bring it into existence—is the essence of the image of God, the *imago*

Dei. Of all God's creations, only humans bear this mark of the Creator. Creativity is a divine gift.

Zechariah and Elizabeth's family and friends were amazed when Zechariah declared, "His name is John." That decision helped create the future. The baby in Elizabeth's arms became John the Baptist, the forerunner of the Messiah. John was obedient to God's call, like his parents, and Jesus called John the greatest human on earth.

> Jesus began to speak to the crowds about John: "What did you go out into the wilderness to look at? . . . A prophet? Yes, I tell you, and more than a prophet. This is the one about whom it is written,
>> 'See, I am sending my messenger ahead of you,
>>> who will prepare your way before you.'
> Truly I tell you, among those born of women no one has arisen greater than John the Baptist; yet the least in the kingdom of heaven is greater than he." (Matthew 11:7, 9-11)

But John was a creator of his own future just like everyone else. He played the hand he was dealt and lived the life of a prophet crying in the wilderness. He chose the strange wardrobe and diet. He chose to preach repentance, baptize sinners, and challenge a wicked king. All of these choices created a future that led to a dungeon, an executioner's ax, and his divine destiny.

God can create anything from nothing, with absolute freedom and endless imagination and vision. Humans can create from something God already made, within the boundaries of our reality, and we are often shortsighted. And yet, people take the stuff around them and employ passion, vision, and skill to transform it into something new and wonderful. The sculptor does it with stone, the musician does it with sound, the painter does it with color, and the photographer does it with light. Every human being does it with time. We take what we have, reshape what we can, discard what doesn't work, and add what we need to pursue our future.

Like any other creative activity, the art of living demands both choice and will. Some choices are conscious and executed with great forethought. Others are taken by reflex and instinct, but either way we make a choice. Without the will to act, a vision of the future remains a hazy dream. A potter can visualize the vessel and choose the lump of clay to make whatever she wants. But she must throw the clay, spin the potter's wheel, wrestle the clay into shape, paint it, glaze it, and fire it in the kiln. If she doesn't, the vessel remains a figment of her imagination.

On the Anvil of Time

John the Baptist was extremely popular. The crowds were immense, his influence powerful, and his fame widespread. No wonder his disciples worried when Jesus came on the scene and the crowds shifted to him. But John wasn't jealous; he was pleased to fulfill his role as preparing prophet. In an encounter with his disciples, John laid out five principles he used to hammer out his future on the anvil of time.

> Now a discussion about purification arose between John's disciples and a Jew. They came to John and said to him, "Rabbi, the one who was with you across the Jordan, to whom you testified, here he is baptizing, and all are going to him." John answered, "No one can receive anything except what has been given from heaven. You yourselves are my witnesses that I said, 'I am not the Messiah, but I have been sent ahead of him.' He who has the bride is the bridegroom. The friend of the bridegroom, who stands and hears him, rejoices greatly at the bridegroom's voice. For this reason my joy has been fulfilled. He must increase, but I must decrease." (John 3:25-30)

First, John displayed divine dependence: "No one can receive anything except what has been given from heaven." The unique boundaries of John's life were his by divine right. He embraced God's overarching narrative for his life and future. His identity, his ministry, and his abilities were uniquely his. All of it was the marvelous gift of an all-wise, loving, and powerful God.

We too have the life we have and not another. We were born who we are, not someone else. We live where and when we live and not in some other place or time. We too are called upon to create lives inside the fences of that reality. Like John, our lives are the marvelous gift of our all-wise, all-loving, and all-powerful God even when life feels more like a burden than a blessing.

Second, John displayed a distinct identity: "You yourselves are my witnesses that I said, 'I am not the Messiah, but I have been sent ahead of him.'" There was only one John the Baptizer. He alone lived that life and claimed that mission. He did not waste time wishing he was someone else. Each person is the unique proprietor of a distinct identity with specific features and circumstances. There is no one else exactly like you. Accepting that truth is the beginning of creating and living a beautiful life.

We alone have the power to create that life. Every life has its own features, unique borders, and resources that result in a singular identity. There never has been and never will be another like it. Accepting that truth is the beginning, not the end, of creatively living the most beautiful and wonderful life we can.

Third, John displayed undeniable purpose. He knew his place in the world. He was "the friend of the bridegroom." That undeniable purpose gave shape, direction, and impetus to his entire life. It fueled the man he became and the legacy he left.

People today have one of three reactions to the notion that God has a purpose for their lives. Some deny that anyone, even God, has the right to tell them what to do. They intend to control and steer their own destiny. Others believe they are created with a purpose, but don't have a clue where to find it. They drift around looking for it, mostly in places it cannot be found. Finally, some embrace their purpose, the boundaries of their lives, and the God of those boundaries. Their distinct identity, purpose, and meaning are found inside the fences of their own backyard. They grow and bloom where they are planted.

Fourth, John discovered joy: "The friend of the bridegroom... rejoices greatly at the bridegroom's voice. For this reason my joy has been fulfilled." At the zenith of his ministry, John watched his fame, influence, and adoring crowds slip away. Most people would have felt angry, hurt, or disappointed. John was happy.

Joy is found in gratitude for God's gifts. Those who create the future with that heart discover deep, undeniable, and permanent joy. Envying the lives of others or demanding to know why God's plan and purposes for our lives aren't what we wish they were robs us of that joy. Deep joy belongs to those who are grateful for the privilege of participating in God's great work in the world.

Finally, John fulfilled his future: "He must increase, but I must decrease." John created his life in accordance with his destiny, not in opposition to it. The portrait of his life was of the bridegroom's friend, not the bridegroom. John came alongside Jesus to assist, and then stepped out of the limelight.

When we live out our purpose, we cooperate with our Creator to achieve our destiny. Fulfilling our divine destiny, doing what God made us to do, satisfies our deepest desires. We aren't limited to a paint-by-numbers design and a few tiny pods of paint. The artist's commission provides general direction, but it doesn't limit the artistic freedom required to create a masterpiece.

Creating the future is hard work. The artist has no greater joy than stepping back and beholding the fulfillment of his vision. We can have no greater joy than living with purpose, fulfilling our dreams, and creating a life of beauty and value. It doesn't get better than that.

The neighbors murmured, "What will this child be?" Your family probably wondered the same thing about you. Perhaps you still wonder what you will become, what your future holds. Perhaps you worry that the best opportunities have passed you by, or that your abilities are not very special. Perhaps you think that God doesn't really care about you or your life.

"What will this child be?" The answer is simple. You are commissioned by the Creator to design a portrait of yourself in gratitude for the gift of life. Let God lead you to the canvas that represents your future. Open your hands as God furnishes you with the perfect brush and palette of paint. And then fashion a masterpiece, rich in vibrant color and undeniable passion that only you can design.

What will you be? What will I be? That is the fourth question the Nativity stories pose to us. It is, of course, a question we ask at baby showers, or when we hold a newborn daughter, or niece, or grandson. But it is not only a question to ponder around a birth. It is, in fact, a question to ask over the course of our lives. We are constantly *becoming*. We are constantly in process. That is true because the human condition is one of change and changeability—but it is particularly true of life with God. Friendship with God is never static.

God is always offering us the invitation to become more like him: to become more merciful, more loving, more generous. God is always offering us the invitation to become more like those saints and heroes of the faith who have gone before us: more prayerful, more committed to people at the margins, more attentive to the flickers and surprising presences of God in our midst. And so this fourth question of Advent—which appears at first blush to be just a question of the nativity—is really a question for the whole of our lives: whom will we become? Will we accept the invitation from the most creative One there is to become more like him? To journey from control to creativity? To allow God to take us on a lifelong process of becoming—becoming more like the Christ whose coming we welcome at Christmas?

Questions

1. *What is the relationship between your past and your future?*

2. *What can we do when our dreams of the future seem lost to the realities of the present?*

3. *Why is ongoing self-evaluation important to building the future of our dreams?*

4. *Is a vibrant spiritual life important to fulfilling your dreams? If not, why not?*

5. *In what ways do other people help us find our way to the future?*

6. *What barriers do you face as you become the person you long to be?*

7. *What parts of your spiritual life are most important to your future?*

8. *Are there spiritual practices or disciplines that help you move from who you are to who you want to be? If so what are they?*

Christmas 2004

W e were all crowded in my sister's house for Christmas Day. Brothers, sisters, aunts, uncles, cousins, parents, and friends filled every nook and cranny. The house overflowed with laughter, love, and the joy of being together.

Even with such a crowd, we still felt Ron's absence in the family landscape. This year we were missing two more faces at the table. My father lost his battle with Parkinson's disease the year before. This was my mother's second Christmas as a widow. And Mark, my miracle Christmas baby, was half a world away serving with the US Marine Corps. I missed my father and son terribly.

Suddenly, the phone rang. It was Mark, the birthday boy, calling from Iraq. Thank God for satellite phones.

Mark's battalion had just withdrawn from a fierce battle in the deadly streets of Fallujah. More than a thousand insurgents had died and no one knew the extent of the collateral damage, the innocents lost in the fog of war. Marines and soldiers were killed and wounded. It was not a Merry Christmas for their families. Christmas would never be the same for any of them.

My family gathered to speak to Mark, laughing and listening as they passed the phone around the room. They celebrated Mark's safety and prayed for his continued protection. Our beloved jarhead had only a few minutes. Lots of marines wanted to call home on Christmas Day to give their families the same reassurance: I'm alive and I'm thinking of you at Christmas. The receiver clicked and the line went silent.

The call was a flash of beauty, and a moment of transcendent joy. Too quickly it was over. Laughter and tears of joy and relief flooded the room. I knew I was a lucky man. I had three outstanding children who filled my heart with pride and joy.

Other families never got that Christmas Day phone call. They mourned their sons and daughters that day and a dark shadow would hang over all their future holiday celebrations. Guilt—real, palpable, inescapable, and overwhelming guilt—inevitably came with the relief of avoiding a tragedy others face.

Life still wasn't fair. But I was very thankful to be among the parents whose children were coming home alive. We would grieve and pray for those who lost a child, a parent, or a spouse to this war. We would thank the veteran and honor his or her service. We would give to charities that helped injured soldiers and cared for the orphans, widows, and widowers of the fallen.

My eyes welled with tears of gratitude. I was so thankful my son was alive. Twenty years after our blue baby was born, God was still sustaining and protecting him. I would not stand over a coffin trying to hold back my tears. His mother would not be handed a precisely folded flag by a somber young marine and thanked on behalf of a grateful nation.

Once again we were given an amazing Christmas gift. Once again we were spared a great agony. I knew it. I just didn't know why. At that moment I didn't really care. I was just glad to be one of the lucky ones. Again.

I still didn't know why.

CHAPTER 5

WHERE IS THE CHILD?

The Magi's Journey from Disappointment to True Treasure

In those days a decree went out from Emperor Augustus that all the world should be registered. This was the first registration and was taken while Quirinius was governor of Syria. All went to their own towns to be registered. Joseph also went from the town of Nazareth in Galilee to Judea, to the city of David called Bethlehem, because he was descended from the house and family of David. He went to be registered with Mary, to whom he was engaged and who was expecting a child. While they were there, the time came for her to deliver her child. And she gave birth to her first-born son and wrapped him in bands of cloth, and laid him in a manger, because there was no place for them in the inn. (Luke 2:1-7)

Gabriel's two birth announcements have been fulfilled. Zechariah and Elizabeth have a son named John, and Mary and Joseph have a son named Jesus. The Gospel of Matthew fills in the rest of the story.

> Now the birth of Jesus the Messiah took place in this way. When his mother Mary had been engaged to Joseph, but before they lived together, she was found to be with child from the Holy Spirit. Her husband Joseph, being a righteous man and unwilling to expose her to public disgrace, planned to dismiss her quietly. But just when he had resolved to do this, an angel of the Lord appeared to him in a dream and said, "Joseph, son of David, do not be afraid to take Mary as your wife, for the child conceived in her is from the Holy Spirit. She will bear a son, and you are to name him Jesus, for he will save his people from their sins." All this took place to fulfill what had been spoken by the Lord through the prophet:
>
> > "Look, the virgin shall conceive and bear a son,
> >
> > and they shall name him Emmanuel,"
>
> which means, "God is with us." When Joseph awoke from sleep, he did as the angel of the Lord commanded him; he took her as his wife, but had no marital relations with her until she had borne a son; and he named him Jesus. (Matthew 1:18-25)

From there, the story moves from the powerless to the powerful as Matthew introduces a group of wise men from the East and King Herod in his Jerusalem palace.

In the time of King Herod, after Jesus was born in Bethlehem of Judea, wise men from the East came to Jerusalem, asking, "Where is the child who has been born king of the Jews? For we observed his star at its rising, and have come to pay him homage." When King Herod heard this, he was frightened, and all Jerusalem with him; and calling together all the chief priests and scribes of the people, he inquired of them where the Messiah was to be born. They told him, "In Bethlehem of Judea; for so it has been written by the prophet:

'And you, Bethlehem, in the land of Judah,

are by no means least among the rulers of Judah;

for from you shall come a ruler

who is to shepherd my people Israel.'"

Then Herod secretly called for the wise men and learned from them the exact time when the star had appeared. Then he sent them to Bethlehem, saying, "Go and search diligently for the child; and when you have found him, bring me word so that I may also go and pay him homage." When they had heard the king, they set out; and there, ahead of them, went the star that they had seen at its rising, until it stopped over the place where the child was. When they saw that the star had stopped, they were overwhelmed with joy. On entering the house, they saw the child with Mary his mother; and they knelt down and paid him homage. Then, opening their treasure chests, they offered him gifts of gold, frankincense, and myrrh. And having been warned in a dream not to return to Herod, they left for their own country by another road. (Matthew 2:1-12)

Sunday school Christmas pageants and television holiday specials tend to distort these searchers into caricatures. But the magi were real people with feelings, needs, and desires. The biblical account does not tell us everything, but what we know opens the door to one of life's most important questions.

After a long, arduous journey, the magi stood at the gates of the king's palace and asked the obvious question, "Where is the child who has been born king of the Jews?" At the end of their search, these sages expected to find what they were looking for. They didn't.

The Message of the Magi

These ancient astronomers saw something rare and special in the night sky. Reading the celestial omens, they concluded that a Jewish king had been born. The star or phenomenon was so spectacular they felt compelled to investigate. Other people—including Herod—peered into the same night sky, but did not see what the magi saw.

The magi left home and took a difficult and dangerous journey to bring incredibly expensive gifts to a baby they didn't know. They were privileged to see his star and fortunate to have the resources to make the trip. They presumed this new King of the Jews would be born in the palace, so they set out for Jerusalem. The star did not lead them to Herod's palace. Their assumptions did. They were wrong.

The journey was the pinnacle experience of their lives. Captivated by their star, the magi did what they had to do to reach their goal. They did not know they were part of the greatest event in human history. If they hadn't pursued their dream, they would have been lost in the archives of ancient history, not celebrated every year at Epiphany.

Like those long-ago wise men, we chase our star. Something captivates us—a career, a goal, an achievement, a dream, or a person. That's our star. When something or someone captivates us we can become its prisoners. Life is defined by its pursuit and it shapes our perspectives.

Their star wasn't just another one of the billions of heavenly lights shining on a clear, dark night. That particular celestial phenomenon held incredible significance and meaning. Other people look at the same panorama of options and possibilities but don't see what we see, value what we value, or choose what we choose. Like the magi we invest our stars with meaning and significance others do not and cannot see.

We chase our dreams because, at a deep and primal level, we believe reaching those goals will fill the great voids deep in our souls. That need drives the pursuit. The sheer varieties of the ways people seek meaning and happiness in life is amazing. But in the end, all human quests are variations on the same theme: the relentless drive to satisfy the inexplicable hunger in our souls.

For Christians that internal hunger confirms a divinely created longing for connection with God. Separation from our Creator leaves us empty and restless and fills us with deep and ever-expanding longings. We look for happiness in possessions, people, or achievements but only God can fill our empty souls. Blaise Pascal observed: "the infinite abyss can only be filled by an infinite and immutable object, that is to say, only by God Himself" (Pascal, *Pensees*, Section 7:425).

We do not live the lives we were created for and we know it. In Genesis 3 we read about the end of man's idyllic life in the garden of Eden. The story of human disobedience and fall from grace holds clues to the nature of our deepest longings. On the day we lost paradise and our intimate relationship with God, a deep and awful chasm opened in the depths of our souls.

When we lost our place in Eden, an intense need for belonging began. When we lost God's presence, an intense need for love and intimacy began. When we lost our purity and innocence, an intense need for justice began. When we lost our work in the garden, an intense need for achievement began. When we lost our sense of purpose, an intense need for significance began.

In this post-Eden wilderness we reach for something to meet these deep, fundamental needs. We hope reaching an elusive goal will bring what we want most: a home where we belong, relationships that heal our loneliness, assurance that good wins over evil, success that is fulfilling, and a reason to live that gives us meaning, significance, and a lasting legacy.

The Long Journey

The magi came from the East. The Bible doesn't say how far east. In various traditions around the world, people believe the magi came from faraway places like India, China, and Ethiopia. Others suggest Middle Eastern areas like Tarsus, Babylon, or Persia (modern-day Turkey, Iraq, and Iran). It's possible they lived fairly nearby in the deserts of Arabia.

Matthew 2:16-18 holds tantalizing clues about how far they had traveled. Terrified by a toddler, Herod decided to eliminate the threat to his throne. He ordered the vicious murder of all male children two years old and younger in Bethlehem and the surrounding area. Life or death was calculated based on the wise men's report of the star's first appearance. That means it's possible they traveled for two years.

The road from dream to reality is long and marked by

difficulties, discouragement, dedication, determination, and discipline. It can take years. It can take a lifetime. Like the magi, we are heroes in our own stories on a great quest and travel far to find the treasure we seek. That journey is not measured in miles but in the transformation of our own lives.

When the magi reached Jerusalem they went to the palace and gained entrance. It must have felt good to finally arrive. Only one thing remained: to meet and worship the child. The baby was their goal and the palace was their destination. They thought the two went together. They didn't.

After all the travel, struggle, and sacrifice there was no baby. Not even a rumor of a baby! Their excitement evaporated and disappointment flooded in. All they endured getting to Jerusalem was wasted. Shock and dismay clouded the magi's faces.

We've all been there and know how it feels. All too often, when we finally get what we want, the treasure isn't there. The completion of our quest may bring momentary elation and pride, but it quickly fades. It doesn't bring the joy, peace, or satisfaction we hoped for. It doesn't last. The restless hunger soon returns and we start looking for something else to fill that empty space.

Unintended Consequences

The magi reached the Jerusalem palace but the newborn king wasn't there. The magi's question, "Where is the child who has been born king of the Jews?" set off a tragic chain reaction. King Herod wanted to know who threatened his throne and his heirs, so he devised a diabolical ruse. Armed with the report from his scholars, Herod sent the magi to Bethlehem. He made them promise to report back when they found the child so he could worship too. He lied.

Herod wanted to kill the baby. He would rather destroy the miracle and extinguish the hope of the world than forfeit his status and throne. Faced with the possibility of someone or something greater, Herod refused to relinquish his life as it was, with all of its problems and stresses and embrace what could be.

Some people live that way. The life they have is the only life they know. When Jesus comes and says, "Follow me," people resist, no matter how compelling his promises seem. They aren't ready to risk what they have to follow someone they do not know into a future they cannot see.

We all confront such moments. Some give up, forever focused on what they lost. People self-medicate substituting something, anything, that makes them feel better or dulls the pain. They jump from one fruitless search to the next. One hobby, one person, or one pleasure gives way to the next in an endless and frantic search for something to fill the void. But the magi found another way.

So can we.

Finding Another Way

It was a critical moment for the magi. They could have given up and gone home. Perhaps they thought about staying in Jerusalem to avoid the public shame of their failed quest. They could have spent their lives bemoaning what might have been. But the magi didn't give up or wallow in self-pity.

Confronted with the greatest disappointment in their lives the magi set off in a new direction. These wise men followed a path that was counterintuitive and contradictory to their culture and times. But in the end the magi found what they were looking for.

On the road to Bethlehem the magi again encountered a star. It led them to a young mother, her child, and the end of their quest. Their journey wasn't just from Jerusalem to Bethlehem. The magi went from painful disappointment to joy-filled amazement. In their story we find five critical steps to seeking and finding what satisfies the hungry soul.

Charting a New Course

First, to find what we seek, we must chart a new course. The magi's goal of finding the newborn king of the Jews wasn't wrong. Their destination was. Satisfying our deepest longings is hardwired into each of us by our Creator. But we often go about it the wrong way. Like the magi, we need a course correction.

First the magi had to admit they couldn't find what they were looking for by following the path they were on. The baby wasn't in Jerusalem and that wasn't going to change even if they waited a little longer, or put in a little more effort, or invested more time or money.

We tell ourselves lies to keep us from admitting the obvious. What we seek isn't where we are looking. We believed all the cultural wisdom, did what we were told, and still got it wrong. The problem may not be our pursuit or performance but the destination itself. No matter how stubbornly we hang on, how long we stay at it, or how much harder we try, we cannot find what we seek where we're looking. It can't be found in wealth, power, pleasure, other people, or achievement. If we follow those well-worn paths we'll end up in the same old desolate places.

It's time to try a new path.

Look for Greater Wisdom

To find what we seek, we need greater wisdom. Herod had a question and needed an answer. The scholars Herod asked opened an ancient, sacred book and discovered greater wisdom there. We too need wisdom beyond our own and greater than our times despite the incredible advances in human knowledge and understanding. We too can open an ancient and sacred book and discover God's eternal wisdom in his revelation to us.

The magi set aside their assumptions and what was most

often true to follow directions from an ancient text to a very unlikely place and a very unusual child. By all the standards of their culture and times they could not possibly succeed by pursuing that path. But they did.

Listen to People Who Know

We find that path in part by trusting wise and insightful people. Herod did not seek advice from his political, military, or financial counselors. He went to the "chief priests and scribes of the people" who knew the answer.

We won't find what we seek by following people who don't know the way. We all look to those we admire and respect, to the mores and values of our culture, and the wisdom of the day for clues. All too often and sometimes too late we discover that no matter how well intended or how widely accepted, we don't find what we're looking for there.

It's better to ask for guidance from people who have found what we seek.

But how to do that? In a media-saturated world where superficial sources of supposed wisdom compete for our time and attention, how can we receive guidance from truly wise people? In two ways, I think. First of all, the history of the church is filled with such people, and many of them left beautiful testimony to the wisdom they learned over a lifetime of faithfulness.

St. Augustine of Hippo, St. Francis of Assisi, Henri Nouwen,

Mother Teresa of Calcutta, and many others—both Catholic and Protestant alike—turned their backs on the power, possessions, and pleasure. They found a superior path that led to the deep peace and treasure they sought. We will be introduced in person to these wise saints when we get to heaven, but in the here and now we can uncover their wisdom through reading. (In fact, Advent can be a good time to dream up a reading plan for the year, to lay in store a devotional text or two written by a hero of the faith, and make a commitment to read a page or two a day in the coming year.)

The second way to benefit from other people's wisdom, of course, is to carve out time to deepen the relationships we already have with wise people in our own communities, neighborhoods, and churches. Every church and neighborhood is home to a wise sage or two, and usually we know who they are because we find ourselves wishing our lives were more like theirs. The hard part is not identifying the sources of the wisdom. The hard part is being truly willing to receive the wisdom—because wisdom from a saint is likely to be the kind of wisdom that shakes things up, unsettles things, and calls us to an unfamiliar path.

Wise saints live quietly and peaceably all around us. How do we find the path of wisdom? Just ask them.

Follow God's Leading

The magi saw a star that went "ahead of them . . . until it came to rest over the place where the child was. When they saw that the star had stopped, they were overwhelmed with joy" (Matthew 2:9-10). The same heavenly phenomenon that started them on their journey led them to the little house in Bethlehem that held their heart's desire. What was true for them is true for us.

God is leading. God "has made everything suitable for its time; moreover he has put a sense of past and future into their minds, yet they cannot find out what God has done from the beginning to the end" (Ecclesiastes 3:11).

A single bright thread is woven through the fabric of all human history: the relentless search for love, joy, and peace. It is the surest proof that eternity is in our hearts. People have examined every conceivable nook and cranny, engaged in every conceivable activity, created every conceivable relationship, and still not found what they're looking for. They have tried asceticism and hedonism, celibacy and sexual promiscuity, wealth and poverty. They have indulged or denied every possible appetite, frantically hoping to find joy. They didn't.

But God put eternity in our hearts too. The only possible solution is to follow the One who created the longing.

Look Where You Can Find

What the magi sought couldn't be found where they looked. All our efforts to find our soul's desire are meaningless if we look in the wrong places.

Jesus lived a completely unexpected life. Everything about

Jesus and his teaching runs counter to the common practice, cultural norms, and accepted wisdom of the world. For millennia people have read his words, scratched their heads, marveled at their beauty, and wondered how anything so out of sync with human experience could possibly be true. It's all upside down. The world doesn't work that way. Maybe that's why so many people see the path but refuse to take it.

Peace and fulfillment come from the state of our souls and interior lives. They rest in selflessness, in relationship with God, and in surrender to divine control. There is nothing wrong with hard work, success, or enjoying life's pleasures. There is nothing wrong with good food, fun, art, or beauty. All are wonderful gifts from a loving God that demonstrate his generosity and grace. They are gifts to be enjoyed but were never meant to fulfill our deepest longings.

Christ's followers are not harsh ascetics who hate the physical world and its sensual delights. They do not believe suffering and deprivation automatically lead to righteousness. Nor are Christians willful hedonists and gluttons who worship the idols of pleasure. Both extremes are ultimately dead ends. Neither leads to the treasure we seek.

Creation is a great gift and blessing to be enjoyed. Like any loving parent, God delights in the joy his children feel when they experience his good gifts. But to give one's life to the pursuit of pleasure is chasing the wind. Meeting needs that are spiritual and eternal by material and temporal means is like trying to draw water from a dry well.

A hearty meal, a beautiful vista, a playful puppy, a loving spouse, or a giggling child are delightful, but they are not the source of ultimate meaning. Distracted from the pursuit of what will truly satisfy, we lose the ability to enjoy these good gifts for what they are. It's far better to worship the God who created all these good and beautiful things. Worship puts us in right relationship with the giver of perfect gifts. It's the only joy-filled way to live.

Herod fell into that trap. Blinded by his power and wealth, he ignored the greater truth, lost sight of what matters most, and made a disastrous decision that brought great misery and grief to the people of Bethlehem. If we're not careful we can do the same thing.

> When Herod saw that he had been tricked by the wise men, he was infuriated, and he sent and killed all the children in and around Bethlehem who were two years old or under, according to the time that he had learned from the wise men. Then was fulfilled what had been spoken through the prophet Jeremiah:
>
> > "A voice was heard in Ramah,
> >
> > > wailing and loud lamentation,
> > >
> > > Rachel weeping for her children;
> >
> > she refused to be consoled, because they are no more."
> >
> > (Matthew 2:16-18)

Staying the Course

In the struggles of life, it's easy to lose our way. The magi stayed on course, ultimately reached their goal, and demonstrated what it takes to travel from disappointment to delight.

The magi showed perseverance. Great accomplishments are marked by perseverance that presses beyond the breaking point. Every failure can become the next step on the road to success. Weary of the road, disappointed with the result, and confronted with a daunting new reality, the magi left Herod's palace and began anew. They persevered in a new direction. So should we.

The magi treasured what they found. The star stopped in the most unlikely place: a little village in the Judean hills. The magi found themselves outside a small, humble cottage—not a king's palace. A simple peasant girl greeted them at the door—not a queen in her finery. A toddler sat alone on the dirt floor—not a pampered royal heir surrounded by servants. Baby Jesus wasn't what they expected. But he was the treasure they sought.

How do we know when we ought to press on or treasure what we have? This ancient story gives us three warnings.

First, recognize true treasure when we find it. All too often people don't recognize the treasures in the lives they already have. A thing of great value, precious and unique, can be overlooked in our frantic efforts. We give up real gold looking for fool's gold.

True treasure doesn't always look like treasure. This toddler in a peasant home was not at all what the magi envisioned when they set out on their journey. But they recognized the young king when they found him. They set aside their old expectations and assumptions to make room for a new treasure beyond anything they imagined. The truest, greatest, and most enduring treasure is often much closer than we think.

Many people reject Jesus because they look at the church and see control and corruption. They find Christians flawed and hypocritical. Priests and pastors betray the faith with greed, misconduct, and abuses of power. They hear Jesus' claim, "I am the way, the truth, and the life" (John 14:6 CEB), and dismiss Christianity as intolerant and exclusive.

They are right. No Christian can deny that churches are full of flawed and failing people. They break biblical commandments and make bad choices. They struggle to emulate Jesus' compassion for the poor and commitment to justice. They are acutely aware of their failures and mistakes. They are weak and frail, broken and hurting. They are like everyone else—except for one thing. They've found treasure.

Dismissing Christ because of the failures of his followers is a terrible and tragic mistake. Like a dirty, old, wooden treasure chest, human frailty obscures the treasure that lies inside. People take one look at the decrepit exterior and decide that treasure couldn't possibly be in there. But it is.

Second, acknowledge the value of the treasure. The value

the magi placed on the future king can be measured by their investment. Their gold, frankincense, and myrrh were incredibly valuable and had been carefully packed and zealously guarded throughout their long journey. Perhaps they were tempted to break into their treasure stash along the way—to borrow a little to make the journey easier. But they didn't.

We invest in God's kingdom by offering our time, talent, resources, and worship. We invest in treasure when we steward God's creation and care for people. That is more precious than gold and a sweeter fragrance than frankincense and myrrh. In the end these investments make us richer.

Third, know when to stop searching. The magi were right to persevere until they found Jesus. But once they found him, their quest was done and they went home (Matthew 2:12). Many people get so distracted by sparkling baubles in life that they give up a treasure of eternal worth. When you finally find what you're looking for, stop looking.

The Greatest Quest

The story of the magi is one of the Bible's great quest stories. But the story of Jesus is history's greatest story of all. His mission statement was to seek and save the lost (Luke 19:10). Jesus was remarkably good at finding treasure where no one else could. It usually got him in trouble with the religious leaders who couldn't or wouldn't understand his mission. They rejected the lost people Jesus found.

In response to their criticism, Jesus told three stories about lost things: a missing coin, a lost sheep, and a wayward son (Luke 15). The meaning of the first two stories is clear: God is like the shepherd anxiously scouring the hills for one lost sheep and the woman frantically sweeping her house looking for one lost coin. God is looking for the lost. God looks for us.

The third story is the well-known parable of a prodigal son and his father (Luke 15:11-31). In this story, we discover that there is plenty of God's love and grace to go around. The salvation of a lost sinner does not mean that a faithful follower is loved any less. God invites everyone to rejoice in the miracle of forgiveness, restoration, and reconciliation. Together these stories teach three great lessons.

First, we are lost and can't rescue ourselves. We cannot find our way and need someone to find us and bring us home. We need a savior.

Second, people who reject their Father end up in a strange country where disaster waits on every side. Left to our own devices we blunder into danger, temptation, distraction, and disaster. It was true for Adam and Eve, and it's still true today. We need God to stay on course.

Finally, God pursues us when we're lost and welcomes us back when we come home. He'll restore what we've squandered. He'll even throw a party!

Jesus embarked on a perilous rescue mission. He left the glories of heaven to live on earth, to find us, and to bring us home to God. The Bible describes Jesus' great journey in several ways. In John's Gospel, Jesus is the eternal Word who participated in creation. Jesus is the Light of the world in human form (John 1:14). In Paul's Letter to the Philippians, Christ's journey is described as transformation from a divine being into a humble servant.

> Let the same mind be in you that was in Christ Jesus,
> who, though he was in the form of God,
>> did not regard equality with God
>> as something to be exploited,
> but emptied himself,
>> taking the form of a slave,
>> being born in human likeness.
> And being found in human form,
>> he humbled himself
>> and became obedient to the point of death—
>> even death on a cross.
> (Philippians 2:5-8)

This is the miracle of the Incarnation. Jesus is not just human. Jesus is God in human form, God living among us as one of us. His journey began in the glories of heaven and took him to that small village. Jesus entered a world of poverty and hardship as a vulnerable infant. He surrendered incredible power to experience the frailties of human life. Loved and honored in heaven, Jesus was hated and despised on earth. He did all this to fulfill his quest, to seek and save the lost.

In those dark days in Jerusalem, it seemed Jesus failed. His treacherous enemies falsely accused him, tortured him, and crucified him. End of story! Except that it wasn't the end. It was all an essential part of his ultimate quest. Three days later Jesus defeated death itself and threw open the gates of the kingdom of God. He cleared away the rubble of sin so that the lost can be found and come home. Anyone who believes can be restored and reconciled to God and anyone can find the treasure they truly seek.

Jesus' quest continues. Christmas and Easter were the beginning. From that day to this, Jesus rescues people of every race, culture, ethnicity, age, and gender and brings them home.

If we seek him, he will find us.

Will you join the magi on the journey from disappointment to true treasure?

Questions

1. *What are people searching for in life? Can you define it in a word or phrase?*

2. *What are some of the common ways people think they will find what they are looking for in life?*

3. *What are some of the barriers we face as we pursue the life of our dreams?*

4. *What role, if any, does our spiritual life play in finding our way to the life we long for?*

5. *What are the risks in pursuing one's dreams?*

6. *What role, if any, do the people in our lives, particularly the people of faith, play in finding our way to the life we long for?*

7. *What are some unusual or nontraditional ways the people of God pursue their dreams?*

8. *Sometimes we fail in our efforts to pursue our dreams. Why does God let us fail? What does God want us to do with those failures?*

9. *In what ways can you help others on their journey?*

10. *What lessons have you learned along the way that could help others?*

Christmas 1998

My sister Linda never remarried after her husband, Ron, died from a cerebral hemorrhage in 1968. She raised her daughter, Wendy, alone and they struggled through the years. Ron's absence was always felt most keenly at Christmas.

Wendy grew into a lovely young woman, graduated from college, and married a great guy named Carl. They wanted children very much, but their first child, a daughter, was stillborn and then they lost their second child, a son. She developed endometriosis and then needed a hysterectomy. It looked like Linda would not be a grandmother and their branch of the family tree would end with Wendy.

One day an adoption agent from another state who heard of them through a mutual friend contacted Carl and Wendy. A baby boy would be born soon and was up for adoption. The birth mother was unmarried and struggled with drug and alcohol addiction. She wanted her child to be adopted by someone in ministry because a pastor's family provided the only foster home where she ever felt loved. Were they interested?

Of course they were interested!

The next days and weeks were a blur of applications, interviews, inspections, approvals, and administrative procedures. Somehow they got everything on the adoption checklist done. It was nothing short of miraculous.

Then the day came and they were on their way. They met the caseworker, the adoption agent, and the birth mother. Then they waited. The first time they took him into their arms and looked into his wrinkled red face, a miracle happened. He had not grown in Wendy's womb and was not Carl's child, but in that instant he became their son. They named him Trenton.

The struggle wasn't over. It took a month to finalize the adoption. There were legal delays and crazy emotional ups and downs. It was just a month but it felt like a year. But the day came when the judge slammed his gavel down and it was official: Trenton was their son. They could finally go home.

It was quite a story.

That Christmas the whole family gathered at my parents' old house to welcome its newest member. Trenton lay in the arms of one of his great-aunts, a living, breathing, squirming symbol of hope in a wet diaper. She gently leaned forward and kissed the baby on his forehead.

"You're ours now, Trenton. You're ours now!" she said in a firm whisper. Her voice and gentle touch etched the truth of our family's love deep into his heart.

With that kiss and promise, she laid claim to the future for all of us. Ron would always be greatly loved and sorely missed. But God had been faithful to Linda and Wendy. God was faithful to Trenton, whose life would be vastly different from the one he was born into. What great and marvelous things lay in store for this special child? God had a plan for Trenton but apparently felt no need to explain it to us.

Life can be unpredictable, marvelous, mysterious, and surprising. Who knows what joys lurk just around time's corner?

LET US GO NOW TO BETHLEHEM

The Shepherd's Journey from Oblivion to Faith

T he Christmas story has a surprising number of angelic appearances. In Luke, the angel Gabriel delivered personalized messages to Zechariah and Mary. In Matthew, an angel of the Lord appeared to Joseph in his dreams and told him to marry Mary, flee to Egypt, and finally to return to Nazareth. The magi were warned in a dream not to return to Herod. But only one angelic appearance involved a full multitude of heavenly creatures. The Gospel of Luke tells us that angels visited some hillside shepherds on the night Jesus was born.

> In that region there were shepherds living in the fields, keeping watch over their flock by night. Then an angel of the Lord stood before them, and the glory of the Lord shone

around them, and they were terrified. But the angel said to them, "Do not be afraid; for see—I am bringing you good news of great joy for all the people: to you is born this day in the city of David a Savior, who is the Messiah, the Lord. This will be a sign for you: you will find a child wrapped in bands of cloth and lying in a manger." And suddenly there was with the angel a multitude of the heavenly host, praising God and saying,

"Glory to God in the highest heaven,
and on earth peace among those whom he
favors!"

When the angels had left them and gone into heaven, the shepherds said to one another, "Let us go now to Bethlehem and see this thing that has taken place, which the Lord has made known to us." So they went with haste and found Mary and Joseph, and the child lying in the manger. When they saw this, they made known what had been told them about this child; and all who heard it were amazed at what the shepherds told them. But Mary treasured all these words and pondered them in her heart. The shepherds returned, glorifying and praising God for all they had heard and seen, as it had been told them.

After eight days had passed, it was time to circumcise the child; and he was called Jesus, the name given by the angel before he was conceived in the womb. (Luke 2:8-21)

The angel's message begins like the others: don't be afraid, I bring good news. Unlike some of our other characters we've studied, the shepherds don't hesitate or falter. They get up to investigate the angel's message. "Let us go now to Bethlehem and see this thing that has taken place, which the Lord has made known to us."

The shepherds move from oblivion to faith. They follow the angel's directions to find the baby. When they arrive in Bethlehem, the baby is lying in an animal's feeding trough, just as they were told. The newborn Messiah looks like one of their children: humble, safe, protected, and loved. The angel's words are true! The shepherds immediately start spreading the good news, first to Mary and Joseph, and then to everyone they encounter. The shepherds are the first evangelists for the good news of the gospel.

Unlike the other characters in the Nativity stories, the shepherds don't question what's happening. They aren't like most of us. When we face suffering, disappointment, tragedy, unfairness, and loss of control, we ask hard questions and expect real answers. These questions can be hard to answer, but we need to wrestle with them.

There is one more question. It doesn't appear in our Matthew and Luke Christmas stories. It doesn't come with a colorful narrative, engaging characters, heavenly visitors, or any of the rich tapestry of the other questions. But it too must be asked and answered—and then asked again.

That question is, So what? Why should we concern ourselves with events that happened thousands of years ago and far away? Why does Christmas even matter?

Some say the Christmas story makes no difference at all in our lives or in history. Humans are just pieces of debris floating on the waves of time. Suffering, betrayal, and injustice are just facts of life. There's nothing more, no bigger picture to worry about. The only thing we can do is float along on that current for as long as we can. Even some of the Bible's ancient Wisdom Literature seems to echo this view. "What do mortals get from all the toil and strain with which they toil under the sun? For all their days are full of pain, and their work is a vexation; even at night their minds do not rest. This also is vanity. There is nothing better for mortals than to eat and drink, and find enjoyment in their toil" (Ecclesiastes 2:22-24).

The writer of Ecclesiastes had seen and done everything. No desire went unfulfilled and no feast was left on the table. Still, his life was meaningless. No matter how delicious the meal, how great the pleasure, or how much he enjoyed the moment, he was always hungry for more. When he added it all up, it didn't add up to much of anything. His life was meaningless.

Most people recoil from that kind of despair. We want to believe that life is more than just dust in the wind. Yet we're afraid to take stock of the few decades we've been given. We don't want to admit how we've squandered our time, energies, and talents.

We're terrified that when we reach the end of our lives, they won't amount to anything.

Why should it matter how we've lived? If we are just the cleverest creatures to climb the evolutionary ladder it shouldn't. Our nearest relatives on the evolutionary family tree don't suffer this affliction. They are born, live, eat, make little apes, fight, and die, and do it all without worrying whether or not they lived meaningful lives.

But regardless of ethnicity and gender or their times and cultures, people long for lives that matter. Different cultures have different answers but they all feel the same need. Until very recently the underlying truth was just as universal and just as unbounded by race, place, or time. People are a special creation and the direct result of divine intervention in the natural order.

Some of the most educated and sophisticated among us reject spiritual answers. Science and technology have replaced the old gods, goddesses, and long-held superstitions. Others believe in bits and bytes of data, not dusty old books.

But the triumph of modern science cannot soothe the ache in our souls. Science has wonderful tools for understanding the what and how of our world. But it was never meant to answer the ultimate questions of why or who. Science fails us when people draw conclusions about spiritual reality based on limited observations of our physical existence.

There is another explanation. People long for meaning and

purpose because God gave us that impulse. We hunger for justice because God is just. We seek truth because God is truthful. We long to create beauty and meaning because we reflect God's creative nature. We long for eternity because we have a future beyond the grave.

If the human race is the product of a divine hand, our incessant longings make perfect sense. This world and life in it are out of phase with his image in us. We were created for something completely different. We are displaced refugees from the realm we long for and were made to inhabit. We instinctively know the deep truth. This world as it now exists, broken and bruised, is not the world we were meant to call home.

Humanity's attempts to satisfy these longings have always failed. Utopian schemes turn out to be far from idyllic. Our best efforts to create just and compassionate societies fail to overcome greed, selfishness, and corruption generation after generation. The inevitable and disturbing conclusion is that we wish for a world we cannot create here on earth.

Personal answers fair no better. Materialism, hedonism, power, and personal happiness ultimately fail to satisfy. So do their opposites: asceticism, stoicism, and self-denial. Despite centuries of experience and millions of examples, people keep traveling these well-worn paths. New generations appear, ignore the lessons of the past, and repeat the same old mistakes.

So why won't we give up on the quest? We can't. These needs

are deeply rooted in our souls. If we want a better world or better lives, we see no option other than to keep trying the only ways we know. But we are swimming against the current of our own fallen nature. If humans could create perfect societies or find personal happiness, wouldn't we have done it by now? We've had more than ten thousand years to figure it out.

Stacked up on one side of this dilemma is the accumulated wisdom of the ages. We want a better world. We think we can create it if we are diligent enough, good enough, and keep the rules well enough. We just need to try harder, be more disciplined, or find our path. There's only one problem. It hasn't worked, doesn't work, and can't get us where we long to be.

On the other side are the implausible biblical stories of a virgin birth, a divine child, a remarkable life, and an unusual death that lasted only three days. The story of Jesus, the Son of God who was fully human and fully divine, is at odds with science, culture, philosophy, and religion. His life comes down to one simple truth: Jesus did for us what we cannot do for ourselves.

We can't get to God, so God came to us. We can't rescue ourselves, so God rescues us. We can't earn what we most long for no matter how hard we try. So he gives it to us. We seek a future beyond the grave. He waits there for us. We seek justice, and he will set everything right in the end. We want to relieve pain, and he comforts us. We can't find the solace we need, so God gives us his grace and peace. By God's divine alchemy, even our suffering works together for our good and God's glory.

This is the gospel, the good news of great joy for all people.

We picture Jesus lying in a manger wrapped in swaddling clothes. We see him wearing a seamless robe walking the Judean hills teaching and healing the masses. We see him on Good Friday, a living sacrifice for our sins. We see him wrapped in a burial shroud and gently carried to a rock-hewn tomb. We see him in a spotless glowing robe conquering sin, death, and the grave in his resurrection on Easter morning.

Jesus is the Father's gift to all who suffer, doubt, long for the future, and search for meaning. Jesus is the gift wrapped in the mystery of divine love...a gift meant to be opened.

The gift is yours. If you'll have it.

Questions

1. *What questions bother you most? Which are most difficult to answer?*

2. *Is it important to question the ways we live life? Why or why not?*

3. *Many people seem to reject spiritual answers to their deepest questions. Why?*

4. *What are the challenges in trying to integrate spiritual wisdom into daily life in our secular society?*

5. *In what ways do people sabotage their pursuit of rich and meaningful lives?*

6. *In what ways do people avoid facing the tough questions of life?*

7. *What impact does failure in our quest have on our lives? On others?*

8. *What are the most significant barriers you face in your search for answers to the urgent and perplexing questions of life?*

Christmas 1954

The year he turned seven, my brother David became very sick. The doctors diagnosed a deadly kidney disease. David was allergic to the only available treatment. If they treated him he'd die. If they didn't treat him he'd die. That December instead of dreams of a Merry Christmas, my parents were haunted by their worst nightmare.

They did the best they could for David's last Christmas. They moved him into their first-floor bedroom and stocked up on his favorite ginger ale. They put the Christmas tree in the corner of the living room so David could see the twinkling lights from his bed. There was nothing more the doctors or my parents could do. We waited for the inevitable.

One night my father stood in the dark outside the bedroom door. My mother knelt beside David's bed, her shoulders heaving and her voice whispering desperate prayers as she surrendered him to God's love and care. Mom stood up, wiping her tear-streaked face on the sleeve of her nightgown. She slipped past Dad in the dark with a gentle touch to his shoulder and went to cry herself to sleep.

It was Dad's turn to keep vigil. Silently entering the room, he sat on the edge of the bed and watched his son's restless sleep. Dad had given up on prayer. He wasn't sure he believed in God anymore.

Sitting in the dark, Dad remembered a recent conversation with his older sister, my aunt Katie. When he told her of David's illness, Katie said plainly, "God still heals."

"God still heals." The phrase echoed in his head. It couldn't be true. But what if it were?

Dad decided to call the preacher from Katie's church and ask him to pray for David. He didn't understand the sudden impulse. He'd resigned himself to the inevitable. He was just desperate.

A few days later the young pastor, his wife, and their little girl came to the house. After they visited a while in the living room, the adults went to the bedroom where David lay. He was getting worse. The doctors' dire predictions seemed to be coming true.

The preacher talked to David for a while and read some Scripture. He pulled a small bottle from his coat pocket. Opening it, he dabbed oil on his fingers, touched David's forehead, and prayed. Dad couldn't remember the exact words or how long the prayer lasted, but he never forgot how he felt when the preacher prayed.

Nothing happened. No bolt from the blue. No voice from heaven. No sudden and dramatic miracle. It was pretty much what Dad expected. He and Mom thanked the pastor and his wife, and escorted them to the door. The pastor assured them that the church would keep praying for David. Dad figured maybe prayer was like chicken soup; it couldn't hurt and made you feel a little better.

But the next morning when Mom collected David's daily urine sample, it looked normal. When she took it to the doctor's office, the staff accused her of bringing a sample from the wrong child! The symptoms that had been evident the day before were gone and never came back. David was perfectly healthy and never had kidney problems again—ever.

Through the winter months David grew steadily stronger. He'd lie on his back in bed and exercise his legs. By spring he was up and around, by summer he was playing softball, and in September he was back in school.

The doctors couldn't explain David's recovery. They shrugged their shoulders and said that sometimes things happened that they didn't understand. They were just glad David was alive and getting better.

The doctors may not have known what happened, but my dad did. Deep in the center of his soul, he knew. God heard their prayers and gave him back his son.

Christmas really is a time for miracles.

ACKNOWLEDGMENTS

I want to thank the many people who helped me along the way: Cody Pelham, who read an early draft and made helpful comments; Shelly Beach; Lorilee Craker; Martie Bradley; and the many family and friends who have read, commented, and corrected various drafts and revisions. I am especially grateful to my agent Ann Byle and Credo Communications. This book would only exist on my laptop if it weren't for Ann. I'm also very thankful for the people of Abingdon Press who helped make this journey a delight.

Finally, I am most grateful for Jesus—He knows why.